Vegetable Gardening

By the Editors of Sunset Books
and Sunset Magazine

Lane Publishing Co. • Menlo Park, California

Two other *Sunset* books make good companion volumes for the home gardener: *Ideas for Cooking Vegetables* and *Home Canning*.

Acknowledgments

For their advice and assistance, we wish to extend special thanks to Gerald F. Burke, Donald Bruce Johnstone, Klaus Neubner, Elmer G. Twedt, and Charles B. Wilson.

Supervising Editor: Patricia Hart Clifford
Research and Text: James W. Wilson

Special Consultants: Kathryn L. Arthurs
Assistant Editor, Sunset Books

Steven M. Cohan, Ph.D.

Joseph F. Williamson
Garden Editor, Sunset Magazine

Design: Cynthia Hanson

Illustrations: Dick Cole

Cover: Photographed by John Flack

Editor, Sunset Books: David E. Clark

Seventh Printing June 1979

Contents

Growing Vegetables Step by Step

Whether you grow a few salad greens in a window box or keep a family supplied with vegetables the year around from a large garden, you'll find that the steps to a successful harvest are basically the same. These steps start on this page and are followed by some different approaches to vegetable growing that you might like to try (container crops and community gardens are two). When you need information on a particular vegetable at the planning or planting stages, turn to the Gardener's Guide section of the book where the major kinds of vegetables are listed in alphabetical order.

1. Find a spot in the sun

When you look for a place to grow vegetables, keep the following considerations in mind:

• Choose a spot in the sun. A successful garden must have at least 6 hours of sun a day — preferably full sun. Most vegetables prefer sun all day. The south and west sides of your yard normally get the most light and heat. In hot desert areas, the plot should have afternoon shade. Winter gardens in mild-climate areas should have full sun all day.

• Find a sheltered location. In windy climates side-yard gardens particularly can be exposed to blasts of wind so strong that growth is retarded or staked plants are knocked over. This is especially true in urban areas where buildings are closely spaced. But if a windy area is the only spot for your garden, use a windbreak made of clear fiberglass to reduce wind without cutting off sunlight.

• Start your garden about 2 feet from house walls. The ground immediately next to most homes (especially new ones) may contain harmful lime that has seeped down from concrete, stucco, or plaster walls, and concrete foundations. The only other solution for this would be to excavate and replace 3 or 4 feet of soil.

• Choose an area handy to the water faucet to avoid dragging around long lengths of hose.

• Avoid low areas that flood during heavy rains. Deep sumps bored into the soil and filled with rocks can sometimes solve the problem of water standing in low spots. Raised beds are another solution (see pages 10–11).

• Look for a plot where air can circulate well; plant diseases thrive in stagnant air. If a cramped space is all that is available, tall, sturdy stakes can carry climbing vines up into the sun and breeze.

• Don't rule out areas with sloping ground, such as banks and hillsides. By taking precautions against erosion and sliding of soil, you can produce as many delicious vegetables there as you would on level ground (see page 27). Soil on a hill, though, is more likely to be shallow or rocky than flatland soil.

• There's no reason to limit your garden to one plot. Small, narrow areas along sunny fences or walls make good locations for climbing or vining vegetables. You also may be able to add small salad crops here and there in beds of flowering plants. Small islands of grass can become excellent sites for vegetable beds. Drive short pegs or posts in the corners of these plots to keep hoses from knocking down the plants.

If you have scouted your property and can't find a good site for a vegetable garden, don't be discouraged. Look around your immediate neighborhood for idle land on which to plant a garden, such as easements under power transmission lines. (Check to see if you need a permit.) Small businesses sometimes have back lots that are eyesores but can be gardened in return for cleaning them up. And some forward-looking cities rent small vegetable plots for modest fees. (See the section on community gardens, page 26.)

2. Make a plan

When you have selected the site for your garden, you'll need to draw up a plan showing which vegetables will grow where. Using a simple scale, such as ½ inch per foot, make a scale drawing of your garden plot. Keep in mind that it's easier to expand your growing space next season than to take care of a garden that is too big.

Make two plans of the same plot: one for cool-season crops and one for warm-season crops. Cool-season vegetables can be planted in the early spring right after the last frost (check the frost dates on page 13), in late summer for fall harvest, and throughout the winter where temperatures are mild.

In hot weather these cool-season plants will bolt, producing premature flowers and seeds instead of the tender leaves, stems, or immature flowers that you want to harvest (the tender roots will become woody). If the weather warms up unexpectedly, shade them with netting or lath held up off the plants by stakes.

Warm-season vegetables need adequate heat to germinate the seed, set fruit, and ripen their crops. With most of these crops, the fruit is what you harvest. If you find that your climate is too cool in summer for the warm-season plants you want to grow, try early varieties — they require less heat to mature than late varieties. Some warm-season vegetables, however, require so many warm days and nights that they rarely succeed in cool climates.

The perennials will come back reliably for several seasons, sending up new growth from heavy, frost-hardy roots. Most perennials should be planted in early spring. Plant them in the back of your plot where they'll be out of the way of the beds you'll be replanting throughout the season.

A succession garden

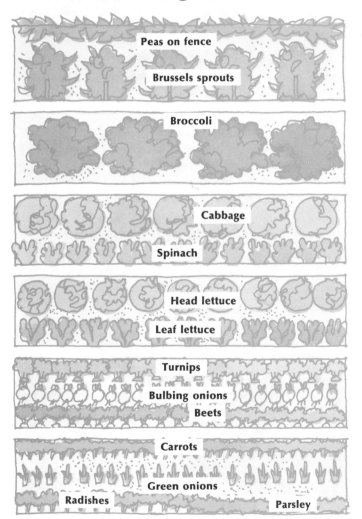

Cool season. *For a continuous harvest, plant part of each row every few weeks during cool weather. To save space, interplant fast growers such as radishes among slow crops such as cabbage.*

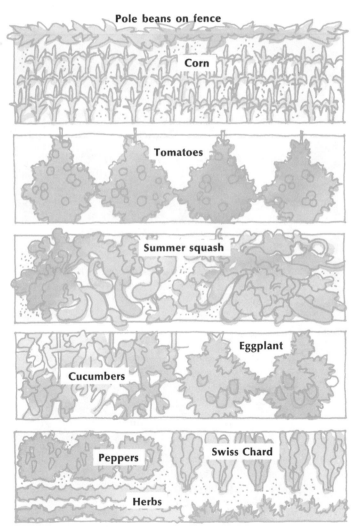

Warm season. *Replace cool-season crops with these after soil has warmed up. Supports for sprawling squash, cucumbers, and tomatoes save space and keep fruit from rotting on wet ground.*

3. Buy seeds

If you're planning your garden in the winter, you'll have time to write for seed catalogs from the companies listed below. Ordering seeds from a catalog gives you a wider choice of varieties than buying seeds from a rack, but if it's time to plant and you haven't ordered seeds yet, buying them in your local stores will be speedier.

Decide at this time, too, which of your crops you'll grow from purchased plants. Unless you want to start some seeds indoors or in a greenhouse, crops such as tomatoes, eggplant, and peppers are more easily grown from plants you buy at a nursery. (These you'll buy right before planting time — see step 6.) Check the Gardener's Guide to find out the best way to start the vegetables you want to grow and make a note on your garden plan.

Do you want hot or mild peppers, small or large tomatoes, bush or pole beans? When you've made these kinds of decisions, check the variety recommendations in the Gardener's Guide section of this book. Vegetable-gardening neighbors, your county agricultural agent, and your own experience will tell you which varieties perform best in your area.

When you read the variety descriptions on the seed packet or in the catalog, look for those qualities that are most important to you. (Some varieties are particularly good for canning, for example.) You'll find superior qualities most often in hybrids since they were bred for special purposes such as a high yield, good flavor, or early harvest. Another sign of quality is an All-America award — varieties that have won this award performed better than other varieties grown for comparison in test gardens across the country.

Most catalogs and seed packets give the approximate row length a packet will sow. Use your garden plan to figure the amount of seeds you'll need and buy only those you can use in one season.

You'll find seed tapes in catalogs and racks. These tapes are easier to plant than individual seeds — you just lay the tape in a furrow and cover with soil. Seeds are evenly spaced and held in place by the tape, eliminating any chance of their being washed away during watering. Seed tapes are sold in spools 10 to 15 feet long.

Seed catalogs to send for

Companies that sell vegetable seeds primarily through retail stores include Ferry Morse, Northrup King, Mandeville King, and Fredonia Seed Co. Following is a list of seed companies that specialize in mail-order sales. Write to any of them for a catalog but those nearest you or in areas with climates similar to yours will be your best bet.

Burgess Seed and Plant Co., P.O. Box 218, Galesburg, MI 49053. Special section on container vegetables.

D. V. Burrell Seed Growers Co., Box 150, Rocky Ford, CO 81067.

W. Atlee Burpee. Write to the branch nearest you: Box 748, Riverside, CA 92502; Box 6929, Philadelphia, PA 19132; 615 North Second Street, Clinton, IA 52732.

DeGiorgi Co., Inc., Council Bluffs, IA 51501. Unusual vegetables.

Farmer Seed and Nursery Co., Faribault, MN 55021. Emphasis on early and cold-resistant varieties suited to northern states. Also a good selection of midget vegetables.

Henry Field Seed and Nursery Co., 407 Sycamore Street, Shenandoah, IA 51602.

Glecklers Seedsmen, Metamora, OH 43540. Unusual vegetables.

Joseph Harris Co., Moreton Farm, Rochester, NY 14624. Emphasis on Northeastern states.

Charles C. Hart, P.O. Box 169, Weathersfield, CT 06109.

J. L. Hudson, P.O. Box 1058, Redwood City, CA 94064. Extensive herb listing.

Jackson and Perkins, 217 Rose Lane, Medford, OR 97501.

J. W. Jung Seed Co., Station 9, Randolph, WI 53956.

May Seed and Nursery Co., North Elm Street, Shenandoah, IA 51603.

Meyer Seed Co., 600 South Carolina Street, Baltimore, MD 21231.

Nichols Garden Nursery, 1190 North Pacific Highway, Albany, OR 97321. Wide selection of herbs and unusual vegetables.

4. Prepare the soil

This step is a crucial one — healthy vegetables depend on a rich garden soil. Skipping thorough soil preparation is like building a house without a foundation.

A good garden soil should have these characteristics:
- Hold enough moisture for plants to grow, yet drain fairly rapidly
- Remain loose and crumbly even in dry weather
- Have ample space for air to circulate and roots to grow freely
- Be easy to work
- Produce good crops with only occasional applications of fertilizer

These kinds of soil usually have a pleasant smell and are full of earthworms.

The chances that this kind of soil exists in your backyard are slim. If your soil drains very slowly when watered and hardens to a crust when dry, it has too many fine clay particles in it. If it dries out quickly and feels sandy, the soil has too many large sand particles in it. Neither of these kinds of soil or combinations of them can provide vegetables with the right amount of nutrients, air, and water for healthy growth and crop production.

The solution for improving all types of soils is the same: large amounts of organic amendments. Organic matter improves the physical structure of the soil to allow a healthy balance of air and water by lightening clay and acting as a sponge in sand. Organic matter is also essential to making nutrients available to plants.

Organic amendments

Because organic material is constantly decomposing, you'll need to replenish the soil before every planting. This will require a great deal of material, so you'll want to establish an inexpensive source. One of the best and the cheapest is homemade compost that uses waste materials from your garden and kitchen. The directions on page 9 show you how to build and maintain a compost pile.

Other good amendments that can often be found free for the hauling are fallen leaves; sawdust; straw; horse, steer, or chicken manure; peanut, rice, or almond hulls; and cannery waste.

Sandy soils benefit most from the addition of spongy materials such as peat moss that hold water and nutrients. Because wood products and hulls absorb less water than other additives, they are the least helpful in sandy soils. Compost and manure are intermediate in value; they supply some nutrients (which the peat moss does not), but they break down faster.

Wood products work best in clay soils because they can physically separate the fine clay particles without holding moisture. Hulls from various crops do the same thing if finely ground or crushed.

If you use a material that is high in carbon and low in nitrogen, such as straw, sawdust, or grain stubble, it will need nitrogen from the soil while it is decomposing. Because you don't want to take this nitrogen away from growing plants, either compost these materials until they are broken down, work the materials into the soil well ahead of planting to give them time to break down (add it in the fall for spring planting), or add a high-nitrogen fertilizer such as blood meal or fish emulsion when you add the fresh material to the soil.

Here are some good amendments you can use:

Manure. All forms of manure make useful soil amendments. They improve soil structure and act as mild fertilizers. Besides horse, steer, and poultry manures, other kinds, such as rabbit and sheep manure, may be available in some areas.

Fresh manure needs to be aged before it is used as a soil amendment, or it will burn plants. Composting is a good way to age it. If the temperature remains high enough, many weed seeds that are usually present will be killed.

Processed steer manure usually comes from cattle feed lots. It's been treated to kill weed seeds. Use it sparingly (add no more than 8 cubic feet per 100 cubic feet of soil)

L. L. Olds Seed Co., P.O. Box 7790, Madison, WI 53707.

George W. Park Seed Co., Greenwood, SC 29647.

Porter & Sons Seedsmen, Stephenville, TX 76401.

Reuter Seed Co., 320 North Carrollton Avenue, New Orleans, LA 70119.

Rocky Mountain Seed Co., P.O. Box 5204, Denver, CO 80217.

Roswell Seed Co., Box 725, Roswell, NM 88201.

Seedway, Hall, NY 14463.

R. H. Shumway Seedsmen, 628 Cedar Street, Rockford, IL 61101.

Stokes Seeds Inc., Box 548 Main Post Office, Buffalo, NY 14240.

George Tait and Sons, Inc., 900 Tidewater Drive, Norfolk, VA 23504. Regional specialties.

Wyatt-Quarles Seed Co., P.O. Box 2131, Raleigh, NC 27602. Varieties adapted to the South.

as a soil conditioner. Some kinds have high contents of soluble salts. Water heavily after sowing seeds or transplanting plants to wash away excess salts.

Poultry manure is full of nutrients and virtually free of weed seeds. It must be aged or composted before you mix it into the soil since fresh poultry manure will quickly burn a newly planted crop.

In arid regions where salt buildup in the soil is a problem, it's probably best to use soil conditioners other than manure.

Peat moss. This is a fairly expensive but excellent soil amendment. Several types are sold. Coarse brown sphagnum or hypnum peat moss is generally superior to sedge peats, which are usually black and extremely fine textured. Most peat moss sold in bales is air dried. Wet it thoroughly before you mix it into the soil.

Wood products. Various wood products, mainly sawdust and bark, are inexpensive substitutes for peat moss. These amendments are sold in bagged, baled, or bulk form (bulk form is the cheapest). You can get these products from commercial firms and sometimes directly from lumber mills or yards.

You can buy wood products either raw or treated. Raw sawdusts rob nitrogen from the soil as they break down, and a few kinds contain materials that can harm some types of plants. For that reason, most commercial products have been treated with nitrogen and allowed to compost to some degree before they are sold. These commercial wood products are generally safe to use for all kinds of plants. If you use raw sawdust, add a nitrogen fertilizer to it and let it compost for a while before you dig it into the soil.

Green manure. A cover crop called green manure grown during the winter will provide organic matter for your soil the following spring. In the fall, plant any of the fast-growing members of the grass family (annual rye grass, barley, or oats) or the legume family (clover, vetch, lespedeza, broad beans, or peas). Lawn grass seeds grow too slowly to be practical.

In the spring, about a month before planting time, till the entire crop into the ground. Though the top growth may be sparse, the well-developed root system will add a substantial amount of organic matter to the soil as it decays.

Soil fertility

The organic matter you add to your soil will provide nutrients in addition to improving the physical structure of the soil. Since different types of organic matter supply varying amounts of nutrients, a soil test is the only way to find out for sure whether your soil has any nutrient deficiencies.

A quick and dependable method for testing is to buy an inexpensive soil test kit at a garden supply store or through a mail-order catalog and follow the directions. Check with your county agricultural agent or the agricultural extension division of your state university for information about other sources of soil testing services.

The most common soil tests will analyze two factors: nutrient content and soil pH.

Soil nutrients. The chart below shows the functions and sources of the three major nutrients plants need: nitrogen, phosphorus, and potassium. The numbers on a fertilizer label refer to the percentages of these nutrients in

(Continued on page 10)

Vegetables need food too

	Nitrogen	Phosphorus	Potassium
What it does	Promotes rapid growth of stems and leaves. Gives plants a deep green color. Especially important for leaf crops. Use a fertilizer high in nitrogen after seedlings are established.	Encourages root formation, flowering, and fruiting. Work bone meal into the soil before planting. When you set out transplants, water them with a high phosphate solution.	Essential to all plant processes. Promotes root growth and seed production.
Signs of deficiency	Older leaves turn yellow and may fall off. Stunted, overall growth, smaller leaves, fewer flowers, and smaller fruits.	Leaves are dull green with purple tints. Plant growth is dwarfed.	Slow overall plant growth. Leaves might have mottled yellow tips and edges; older leaves look scorched at the edges.
Signs of too much	Plants grow too fast and become weak and spindly. Flowers and fruit come too late in their season.	Little danger of too much phosphorus or potassium.	
Organic sources	Blood meal Hoof and horn meal Cottonseed meal Fish meal, fish emulsion Animal manures Bone meal	Bone meal Phosphate rock	Granite dust Pulverized granite Potash rock Wood ashes

How to make compost

The purpose of composting is to turn the waste materials from your garden and kitchen into a rich, organic soil-conditioning material. A compost pile does this efficiently by accelerating the natural processes that occur when dead leaves, grasses, and other materials decompose. Piling organic materials up while they decay is better than digging them into the ground because, when piled up, they don't temporarily rob growing plants of available nitrogen while breaking down.

What you put in your compost pile will depend on the waste materials available from your garden and kitchen, but you should follow a few basic rules so you don't create a trash pile.

• Spread a layer of plant material, such as fallen leaves, green or dry weeds, and grass clippings, on a flat piece of cleared ground. Add layers of manure (or a few handfuls of a nitrogen-rich fertilizer), topsoil, and kitchen scraps (except meat, fat, and bones). Keep adding more layers until you've used up all the debris. Don't put too much of one material in the same layer or it will tend to pack together, slowing the breakdown and causing odor.

• Chop or grind materials into small pieces before you add them to the pile. Smaller particles offer more surfaces for decay organisms to work on. Materials such as grass clippings that are very fine, however, should be mixed with coarser pieces so they don't turn into a slimy mass.

• Heat buildup is essential to composting. Too shallow a pile won't hold enough heat in, and breakdown will be slower. A compost pile 4 to 6 feet high will hold heat well and let air circulate. Some kind of bin will make it easier to stack compost to this height; see illustrations at right for ideas. Steam rising from the pile is a sign that heat is being generated.

• Keep the pile moist but not soggy. Too much water limits the air supply. A pile with a slightly concave shape will catch and hold the moisture better. During prolonged periods of heavy rainfall, cover the pile with a plastic sheet or tarp to keep it from becoming soggy. If it does get too wet, frequent turning will restore it to a healthy condition.

• Turn the pile every few weeks. Good air circulation discourages odor and flies and speeds decay. Turning also moves the outer, undecomposed material into the center so it can break down. Plenty of succulent material, such as lawn clippings and soft green weeds, should be well mixed with dry or woody materials.

• Nitrogen is needed by the decay-producing bacteria. Periodically include in the layers such nitrogen sources as fresh manure, blood meal, or commercial fertilizers.

• Compost is ready to use when it is crumbly and the original materials have decomposed beyond recognition—usually about 3 months after the heap is built. Sift the compost before you use it to eliminate large, undecomposed chunks.

1" x 2"

Netting

Fence

Top. *Netting helps keep flies from compost pile. This enclosure made of 1 by 2s uses a fence as a fourth side; bin could also stand alone.* **Bottom.** *Circle of welded wire holds shredded compost. After a week wire can be lifted to leave a firm stack and used to hold next pile.*

the product; for example, 5-10-10 contains 5 percent nitrogen, 10 percent phosphorus, and 10 percent potassium.

To get vegetables off to a fast start, work a fertilizer high in phosphorus into the soil when you prepare it. When you set out transplants, water them with a high-phosphate solution. After seedlings are well established, feed them with a nitrogen-rich fertilizer to speed their growth.

The fertilizers listed on the nutrients chart are organic fertilizers and need to be worked into the soil to be effective. Inorganic fertilizers do not improve the soil structure as organic fertilizers do, so they should not be used in place of organic materials. However, for the short term they have two advantages. Most are available faster than organic fertilizers for plants to use. And they are usually less expensive, since they are more concentrated and you apply a smaller amount. Check labels for a fertilizer recommended for vegetables and apply according to label directions. Avoid fertilizer contact with foliage and take care not to overfertilize.

Once you get your soil built up with compost and other organic materials, your need for the inorganic fertilizers should diminish.

Soil pH. The soil pH test will tell you whether your soil is too acid or too alkaline by measuring the hydrogen ion concentration on a scale of 1 to 14. (pH 7 is neutral; any pH less than 7 is acid; any pH greater than 7 is alkaline.) The ideal vegetable garden soil is slightly acid to neutral (pH 6 to 7), but you can grow excellent crops on slightly alkaline soil (pH 7 to 8). A reading at either extreme means that plant roots won't be able to absorb nutrients from the soil.

Ground limestone is effective in counteracting acidity — the calcium in the limestone neutralizes acids. It's usually necessary to reapply limestone every 2 to 3 years, but don't add any lime unless your soil test reading is below pH 5.5.

If you can find it, use dolomitic lime, which contains both calcium and magnesium. Avoid hydrated or burned lime; their caustic action can easily burn your skin, and they leach away rapidly.

A soil with a pH reading higher than 7 is most common in arid regions. Natural causes of alkalinity include low rainfall, poor drainage, and native limestone deposits. Often alkaline soils are also too salty. In extreme cases heavy white or brown salt deposits are left on the soil surface by evaporating water. Salt problems are made worse when softened or brackish water is used for irrigation and when fertilizers with a high salt content, such as manure, are spread.

Because soils usually turn alkaline for more than one reason, you may have to do several things to correct the problem. To reduce alkalinity on well-drained land, flood the soil for 24 to 48 hours to wash excess mineral salts down below the root zone. Counterbalance any slight remaining alkalinity by feeding plants with an acid-type fertilizer. However, if moderate alkalinity remains after leaching, add substantial amounts of acidic amendments, such as peat moss, ground bark, or sawdust to the soil.

On poorly drained land where alkalinity is often most severe (pH reading of more than 8.5), treatments are complex and costly. To avoid the problem entirely, garden in raised beds or containers filled with good garden soil brought in from another area.

Dig it in

When your amendments are ready to go into the soil, keep two points in mind:
• Think *big* when you add organic material — 25 to 50 percent of the amount of soil you're preparing.
• Think *deep* when digging the material into the soil — rototilling will loosen the top layer of hard soil, but only a shovel will go deeper.

If your soil has been gardened before and is fairly loose, digging 3 to 6 inches of organic matter to a depth of 9 to 12 inches should suffice. If your soil is very poor or has never been worked, two solutions to problem soils that require more work but will give you better results are double digging and raised beds.

Double digging. This technique demands a lot of digging, but the resulting mounded beds produce vegetables that are worth it. Follow the steps shown at right; then let the bed settle. After a couple of days, break up the large clods and work the soil into a fine texture. Double digging is the basis for the French intensive method of gardening which allows closely spaced planting in the richly amended beds.

Raised beds. Planting beds raised above the soil level can help you overcome many obstacles to growing vegetables successfully. If your soil is hard and infertile and drains poorly, raised beds allow you a fresh start with a light, rich soil mix (especially good for root crops). If gophers are a problem, you can line the bottom of the bed with 1-inch chicken wire to keep them out. Snails and slugs are often intimidated by the bed, and any pests that do get in are isolated and easier to control. Watering, weeding, and cultivating all require less stooping. Water only goes to the productive areas of the garden, keeping paths and your feet dry. As a bonus, the raised soil tends to warm up faster in the spring, resulting in earlier crops. If you cover the bed with clear plastic or panes of glass, you have a coldframe for protecting tender plants.

The simplest raised bed uses 2 by 12-inch redwood boards reinforced at the corners. Stakes driven into the ground and nailed midway on the boards support the walls. Drainage holes filled with gravel at the bottom of the bed will eliminate standing water. A good width for the bed is 4 or 5 feet; the center of a wider bed would be hard to reach. The length can vary to fit the garden. If you build more than one bed, leave room for a wheelbarrow to pass between them.

Fill the bed with a rich, light soil mix — such as equal parts peat moss, compost, and topsoil. Soak the bed before planting so the soil will settle to about 2 or 3 inches below the top of the bed. If you wait to soak the soil until after planting, many plants will sink and need replanting. Replenish the nutrients by adding organic material, such as rotted manure, at replanting time.

Two solutions for problem soil:
1. Double digging

a. *Cover planting area with compost. Dig one spade's depth; set it aside. Loosen one spade-depth more.*

c. *Finish bed by filling last trench with soil dug from first trench. Bed will be mounded and aerated. Rake fine before planting.*

b. *Use soil from second trench to fill first one; repeat down the bed. Loosen bottom soil each time.*

d. *Thin seedlings or set out transplants in staggered lines so outer leaves of mature plants will just touch.*

2. Raised beds

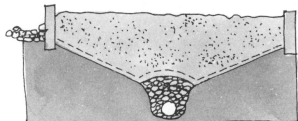

If water won't drain through soil below raised bed, slope soil to a trench running down center of bed. Draintile covered with crushed rock runs along bottom of trench, as shown in cross section. Chicken wire (dotted line) keeps out gophers.

Box made of 2 x 12 redwood boards mitered and nailed together at corners is reinforced by wooden wedges nailed into corners. To support walls, cut stakes about 18 inches long and drive into ground around inside perimeter of bed. Nail stakes to boards.

5. Plant the seeds

It's early spring, your seeds have arrived, and your soil is ready. Before tearing open the seed packet, you'll want to consider two factors to help schedule your planting.

• Method of planting. Those crops that are difficult to sprout outdoors or require a long growing season should be planted indoors or purchased as transplants at a nursery. Others can be sown outdoors directly in the ground. The Gardener's Guide will give you the recommended method for planting each vegetable.

• Time to plant. Check the frost dates for your area on the table on page 13—you'll want to sow your vegetables so they will mature between these dates. Check the Planting Chart on pages 75-78 for the time of the year that is recommended for planting each vegetable.

To start seeds early

You'll find the materials for starting seeds early at a nursery, in seed catalogs, or in your home. Or look for seed starting kits that include all the materials in one package. Here are the basics:

• Sterilized potting soil
• Milled sphagnum moss or vermiculite
• Containers with holes for drainage in the bottoms (see illustrations below)
• Peat pots (2½ to 3-inch diameter), peat pellets, growing cubes, or paper cups with holes in the bottom
• Plastic bags

Follow these steps for planting the seeds. If you are not sowing a large quantity of seeds, you can eliminate a

Indoor seed starters

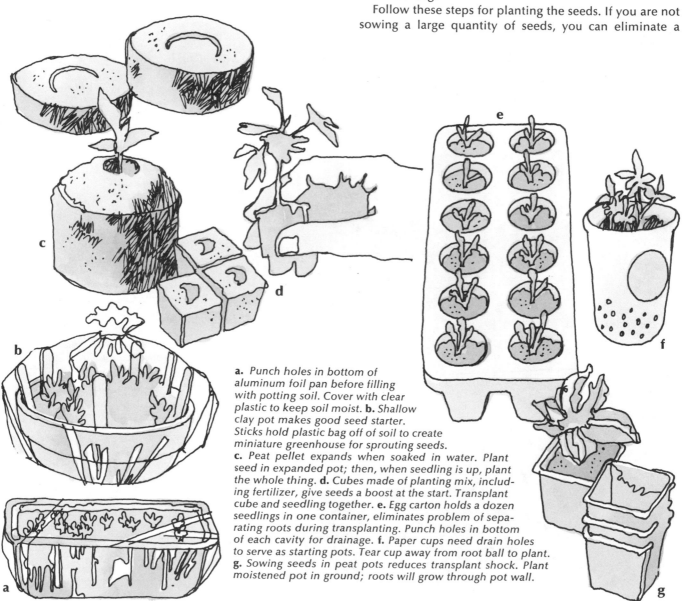

a. Punch holes in bottom of aluminum foil pan before filling with potting soil. Cover with clear plastic to keep soil moist. b. Shallow clay pot makes good seed starter. Sticks hold plastic bag off of soil to create miniature greenhouse for sprouting seeds. c. Peat pellet expands when soaked in water. Plant seed in expanded pot; then, when seedling is up, plant the whole thing. d. Cubes made of planting mix, including fertilizer, give seeds a boost at the start. Transplant cube and seedling together. e. Egg carton holds a dozen seedlings in one container, eliminates problem of separating roots during transplanting. Punch holes in bottom of each cavity for drainage. f. Paper cups need drain holes to serve as starting pots. Tear cup away from root ball to plant. g. Sowing seeds in peat pots reduces transplant shock. Plant moistened pot in ground; roots will grow through pot wall.

transplanting step by sowing seeds directly in a peat pot or paper cup instead of a flat or tray.

- Fill the container with the soil mix ½ inch from the top and firm it level.
- Sow seeds at the depth and spacing given on the Planting Chart (pages 75-78) or on the seed packet.
- Cover the soil with the moistened sphagnum moss or vermiculite.
- Set the containers in a sinkful of water up to their rims until the soil surface is moist.
- Let the containers drain and place them in plastic bags that you have perforated for ventilation.
- Place out of direct sunlight where the temperature is 70 to 75°F. (See page 14 about providing heat.)

As soon as the seeds have sprouted, remove the plastic bags and set the containers beside a sunny window.

If nights become very cold, however, move the containers away from the glass. Continue to keep the soil moist but not drenched.

Once the seeds have sprouted, a product made for starting transplants will stimulate healthy root and foliage growth. Use according to label directions.

If you have planted a quantity of seeds in a tray or flat, the seedlings are ready for transplanting after the second set of leaves appears. Holding each seedling by the stem, place it in a pot at the same depth it was grown in the tray (tomatoes or very leggy plants can be planted up to the bottom set of leaves).

The plastic over the seed container creates greenhouse-like conditions. If the seeds you are starting require soil temperatures over 70°F. (see the Planting Chart, pages 75-78), artificial light or a hotbed will provide the extra

Plan your growing season around frost dates

Based on U.S.D.A. weather records

State	Last in Spring	First in Fall	State	Last in Spring	First in Fall	State	Last in Spring	First in Fall
Alabama, N.W.	Mar. 25	Oct. 30	Kentucky	Apr. 15	Oct. 20	N. Dakota, E.	May 16	Sept. 20
Alabama, S.E.	Mar. 8	Nov. 15	Louisiana, No.	Mar. 13	Nov. 10	Ohio, No.	May 6	Oct. 15
Arizona, No.	Apr. 23	Oct. 19	Louisiana, So.	Feb. 20	Nov. 20	Ohio, So.	Apr. 20	Oct. 20
Arizona, So.	Mar. 1	Dec. 1	Maine	May 25	Sept. 25	Oklahoma	Apr. 2	Nov. 2
Arkansas, No.	Apr. 7	Oct. 23	Maryland	Apr. 19	Oct. 20	Oregon, W.	Apr. 17	Oct. 25
Arkansas, So.	Mar. 25	Nov. 3	Massachusetts	Apr. 25	Oct. 25	Oregon, E.	June 4	Sept. 22
California			Michigan, Upper pen.	May 25	Sept. 15	Pennsylvania, W.	Apr. 20	Oct. 10
Imperial Valley	Jan. 25	Dec. 15	Michigan, No.	May 17	Sept. 25	Pennsylvania, Cen.	May 1	Oct. 15
Interior Valley	Mar. 1	Nov. 15	Michigan, So.	May 10	Oct. 8	Pennsylvania, E.	Apr. 17	Oct. 15
Southern Coast	Jan. 15	Dec. 15	Minnesota, No.	May 25	Sept. 15	Rhode Island	Apr. 25	Oct. 25
Central Coast	Feb. 25	Dec. 1	Minnesota, So.	May 11	Oct. 1	S. Carolina, N.W.	Apr. 1	Nov. 8
Mountain Sections	Apr. 25	Sept. 1	Mississippi, No.	Mar. 25	Oct. 30	S. Carolina, S.E.	Mar. 15	Nov. 15
Colorado, West	May 25	Sept. 18	Mississippi, So.	Mar. 15	Nov. 15	S. Dakota	May 15	Sept. 25
Colorado, N.E.	May 11	Sept. 27	Missouri	Apr. 20	Oct. 20	Tennessee	Apr. 10	Oct. 25
Colorado, S.E.	May 1	Oct. 15	Montana	May 21	Sept. 22	Texas, N.W.	Apr. 15	Nov. 1
Connecticut	Apr. 25	Oct. 20	Nebraska, W.	May 11	Oct. 4	Texas, N.E.	Mar. 21	Nov. 10
Delaware	Apr. 15	Oct. 25	Nebraska, E.	Apr. 15	Oct. 15	Texas, So.	Feb. 10	Dec. 15
District of Columbia	Apr. 11	Oct. 23	Nevada, W.	May 19	Sept. 22	Utah	Apr. 26	Oct. 19
Florida, No.	Feb. 25	Dec. 5	Nevada, E.	June 1	Sept. 14	Vermont	May 23	Sept. 25
Florida, Cen.	Feb. 11	Dec. 28	New Hampshire	May 23	Sept. 25	Virginia, No.	Apr. 15	Oct. 25
Florida, South of Lake Okeechobee, almost frost-free			New Jersey	Apr. 20	Oct. 25	Virginia, So.	Apr. 10	Oct. 30
Georgia, No.	Apr. 1	Nov. 1	New Mexico, No.	Apr. 23	Oct. 17	Washington, W.	Apr. 10	Nov. 15
Georgia, So.	Mar. 15	Nov. 15	New Mexico, So.	Apr. 1	Nov. 1	Washington, E.	May 15	Oct. 1
Idaho	May 21	Sept. 22	New York, W.	May 10	Oct. 8	W. Virginia, W.	May 1	Oct. 15
Illinois, No.	May 1	Oct. 8	New York, E.	May 1	Oct. 15	W. Virginia, E.	May 15	Oct. 1
Illinois, So.	Apr. 15	Oct. 20	New York, No.	May 15	Oct. 1	Wisconsin, No.	May 17	Sept. 25
Indiana, No.	May 1	Oct. 8	N. Carolina, W.	Apr. 15	Oct. 25	Wisconsin, So.	May 1	Oct. 10
Indiana, So.	Apr. 15	Oct. 20	N. Carolina, E.	Apr. 8	Nov. 1	Wyoming, W.	June 20	Aug. 20
Iowa, No.	May 1	Oct. 2	N. Dakota, W.	May 21	Sept. 13	Wyoming, E.	May 21	Sept. 20
Iowa, So.	Apr. 15	Oct. 9						
Kansas	Apr. 20	Oct. 15						

Allow 10 days either side of above dates to meet local conditions and seasonal differences.

warmth. For all other seeds, a coldframe or some kind of cover over the seedbed will protect them from cold nights and loss of moisture.

Artificial light. Since all seeds are covered with some soil at planting, light from the sun or from fluorescent lamps serves mostly to provide heat. Light becomes necessary for photosynthesis and growth as soon as the first sprout shows above the soil.

Fluorescent lamps above the plant can provide both heat for sprouting seeds and light to grow seedlings. Certain kinds of fluorescent lamps are especially made for growing plants; these lamps concentrate more energy in the red and blue areas of the light spectrum. They are more expensive than ordinary fluorescent lamps, but they hasten seed germination and seedling growth.

In sprouting seeds, use the gentle warmth and radiant energy from the tubes by positioning seed pans only 3 or 4 inches below the tubes. Burn the tubes constantly until the sprouts have emerged; then give the young sprouts 12 to 16 hours of light daily.

Once seeds have sprouted, they will grow into compact seedlings under temperatures of 60 to 65°F. Place the seedlings no more than 12 inches below the tubes. At greater distances from the light source, light intensity falls off drastically, causing seedlings to become leggy.

Coldframes. A coldframe is a low-profile structure with a slanting, transparent roof that provides a protected area for early spring and late fall growing. Simple to construct, these devices are useful during most of the year. Coldframes capture solar heat during the day and hold some of it through the night, protecting plants against frost damage. Since the coldframe is heated by the sun, slant it toward the south and paint the interior white to reflect sunlight onto the plants. When temperatures drop below 32°F., the frame should be covered with a tarp or plastic film. On warm days, cool the bed by raising the sash.

Cover the floor of the coldframe with fast-draining sand. A light potting mix on top of this should be 3 inches deep for sowing seed. If you sow seed in flats, raise the flats off the floor by setting them on blocks.

Hotbeds. When you bury electric cables in the floor of a coldframe, you have a hotbed that is especially useful for hard-to-germinate seeds. (Use heating cables made for this purpose.) Incandescent bulbs are less satisfactory heat sources because they have little effect on soil temperature. Digging fresh manure into the soil beneath a coldframe is another method of providing heat.

When electric cables are used to heat hotbeds, you can sow seeds in the soil directly above them; in fact,

If you don't have a greenhouse, try these...

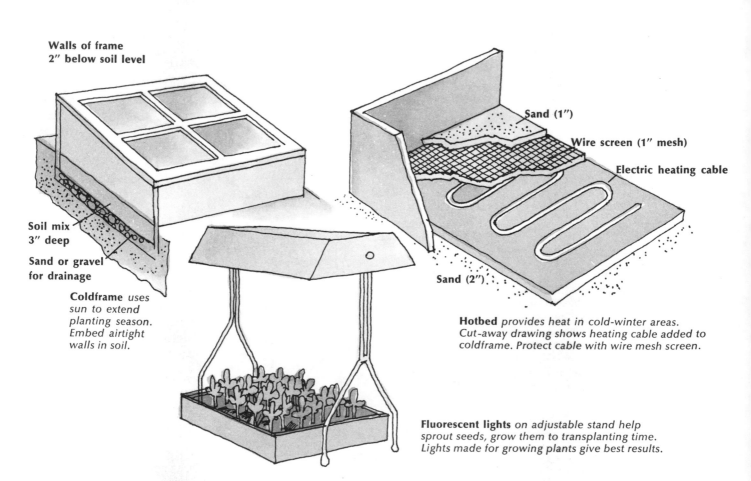

Walls of frame 2″ below soil level

Soil mix 3″ deep

Sand or gravel for drainage

Coldframe *uses sun to extend planting season. Embed airtight walls in soil.*

Sand (1″)

Wire screen (1″ mesh)

Electric heating cable

Sand (2″)

Hotbed *provides heat in cold-winter areas. Cut-away drawing shows heating cable added to coldframe. Protect cable with wire mesh screen.*

Fluorescent lights *on adjustable stand help sprout seeds, grow them to transplanting time. Lights made for growing plants give best results.*

some gardeners grow winter crops of vegetables this way. Most gardeners, however, use hotbeds first for sprouting seeds and later, without heat, as coldframes for growing seedlings to the size for transplanting to the garden. Cover floors of hotbeds with fast-draining fine gravel or sand, providing a clean area for placing flats and pots and for evaporating moisture to raise the humidity.

Where winters are severe, pile up earth around hotbeds to give more insulation. Covers made of two layers of glass or plastic with an air space between will decrease loss of heat by radiation.

Covered seedbeds. A number of useful devices are based on the principle of the coldframe. European gardeners have long used cloches, interlocking A-frame glass canopies with closed ends, over rows of seedlings (mainly frost-tender leafy types) to add growing time to both ends of the season and to protect warmth-loving vegetables. Most cloches are held in wire carrying frames and can be taken apart for storage. Modern cloches employ sheet plastic over wire hoops. Bury the edges of the plastic in the soil. Open both ends of the shelter on warm days to prevent vegetables from literally becoming cooked.

Individual bonnets of heavy wax paper can be placed over single seedlings. The caps trap solar heat and speed growth, as well as protect plants from frost damage. No covering can protect against extreme cold, though, so don't set warmth-loving plants in the garden until all heavy frosts are past.

To sow seeds outdoors

Getting seeds to sprout that you sow in the ground depends on four factors:

• Soil temperature. Seeds will rot if they're planted too early, so check the Planting Chart, pages 75–78, for the correct soil temperature of the crop you're planting. Figuring the soil temperature to lag about 2 weeks behind air temperature will give you a rough guide; to be more accurate you'll need to buy a soil thermometer.

• Planting depth. Seeds planted too deep may not reach the soil surface. Check the Planting Chart or the seed packet for the correct depth — it's always about three times the diameter of the seed.

• Soil condition. Soil should be raked fine so it's free of lumps or clods that will keep seeds from sprouting.

• Soil moisture. The right amount of water keeps seeds moist but not soggy and keeps crusts from forming on top of the soil. Use a fine mist spray or perforated soaker to water so seeds don't wash away. For tiny seeds that dry out quickly — such as carrot seeds — cover the seed row with clear plastic to help keep the moisture in. Remove it as soon as the seeds sprout. You could also use a mulch for the same purpose, especially in hot weather.

After your soil has been prepared, rake it level so water won't run off. For large vegetables such as corn, squash, or tomatoes that will need soaking, make furrows or basins before you plant (see illustrations at right). Crops sown by broadcasting can be watered by sprinkler.

Three ways to sow seeds outdoors

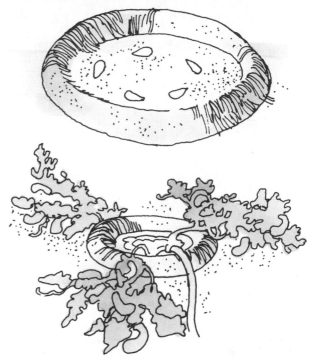

Planting vining squash *in circles called hills gives roots room to spread out, makes a basin for efficient watering. Plant five seeds in a 12 to 18-inch circle and thin to three plants.*

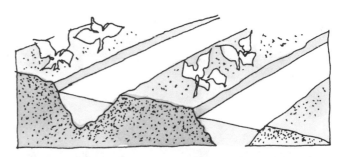

Make furrows *for watering between rows before planting for large vegetables that need deep soaking. Smaller furrows for smaller crops will fill in and need rehoeing.*

Broadcasting *takes a steady hand to spread seeds evenly. Use this method to sow wide bands or the beds shown on page 11.*

6. Buy and set out plants

The object in transplanting is to shock the plant as little as possible — any sudden change in environment can cause growth to slow down and the plant may never recover. Chances for success increase if you can choose a healthy plant from the nursery. The plant on the left will adjust to transplanting much better than a plant that has any of the problems of the plant on the right.

Check the Planting Chart (pages 75–78) for the best time to set out each vegetable. Plants that you have raised indoors and some plants from the nursery come from greenhouselike conditions and need to be gradually accustomed to the outdoors before transplanting by a process called hardening-off. Set plants out on a warm day and gradually work up to leaving them out overnight. After several nights outdoors in their containers, plants should be ready to go into the garden.

Try to disturb the roots as little as possible during transplanting. Peat pots have the advantage here since you can plant the entire pot. Follow these steps for setting out purchased or home grown plants:

- Dig holes for receiving the plants and fill them with water; let it soak in.
- Water plants thoroughly. If you are using peat pots, soak them until they are moist and soft before you set them out; then break off the upper edge of the pot so it's even with the soil line.
- If the plants are not in individual pots, carefully separate the root ball of each plant from the larger soil mass, preserving as much soil around the roots as possible. If a plant in an individual pot is rootbound, rough up the roots with your fingers before planting. Trim off any roots that are very long.
- If the plants are quite large, trim off about half the leaves to reduce the loss of water. Don't trim the central growing tip.
- Until they are planted, cover roots with a damp cloth to prevent them from drying. Even brief drying can damage delicate feeder roots.
- Set in the plants to the original depth or *slightly* deeper than they grew in the soil. Planting too deep can slow or stop plant growth. Tomatoes and very leggy plants as shown below are exceptions — you can bury from half to three-quarters of their stems.
- Cover the roots with loose soil drawn up around them and gently firmed down. Tug at the tip of a leaf. If the plant stirs, firm the soil again. The leaf tip should come off in your fingers before the plant will move. Don't mound the soil up, though, or it will shed water.
- Water again to settle the soil around the roots. If you haven't added a high-phosphate fertilizer during soil preparation, use a high-phosphate starter solution to aid in root formation.
- Protect transplants from extreme hot or cold weather and from pests such as cutworms and snails by using one of the devices illustrated on the opposite page. Open plastic coverings on warm afternoons.

Choosing a nursery plant

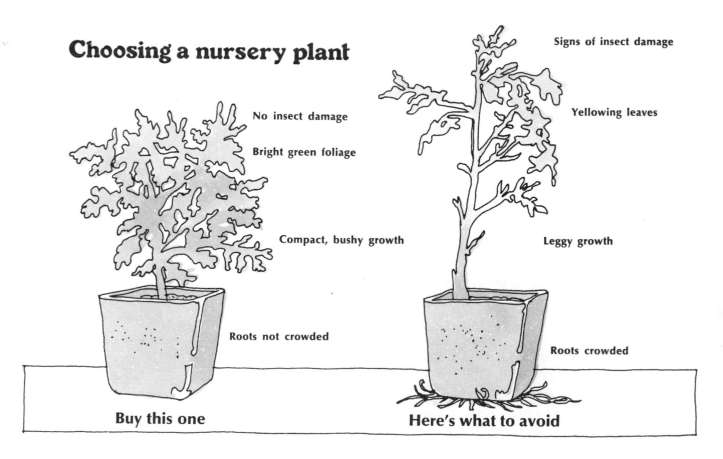

No insect damage

Bright green foliage

Compact, bushy growth

Roots not crowded

Buy this one

Signs of insect damage

Yellowing leaves

Leggy growth

Roots crowded

Here's what to avoid

Protecting transplants: six ideas

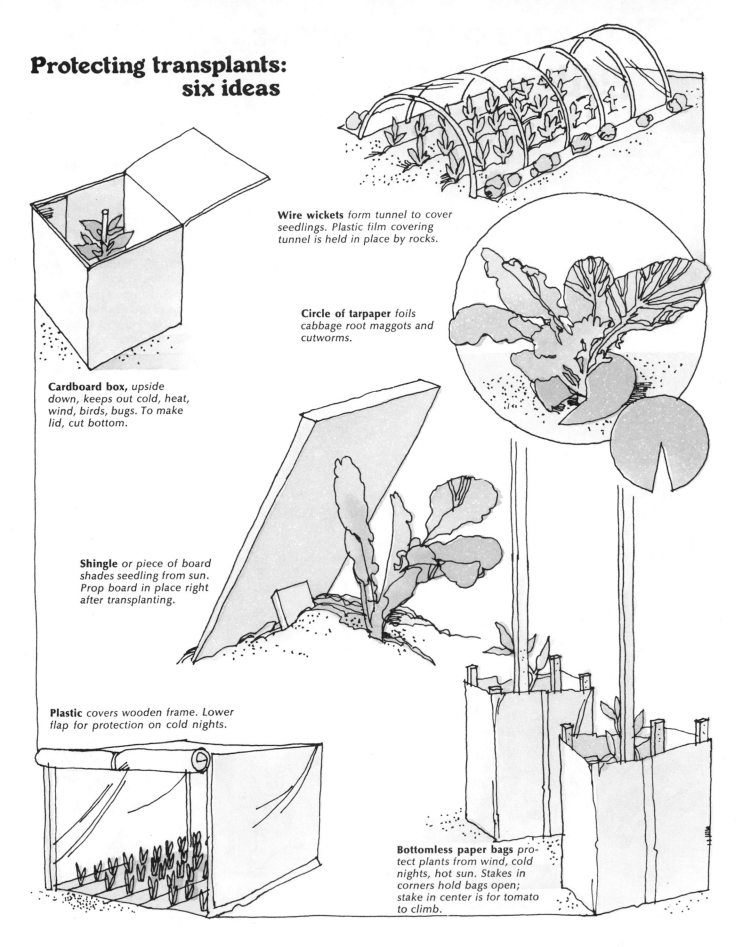

Wire wickets *form tunnel to cover seedlings. Plastic film covering tunnel is held in place by rocks.*

Cardboard box, *upside down, keeps out cold, heat, wind, birds, bugs. To make lid, cut bottom.*

Circle of tarpaper *foils cabbage root maggots and cutworms.*

Shingle *or piece of board shades seedling from sun. Prop board in place right after transplanting.*

Plastic *covers wooden frame. Lower flap for protection on cold nights.*

Bottomless paper bags *protect plants from wind, cold nights, hot sun. Stakes in corners hold bags open; stake in center is for tomato to climb.*

7. Take care of your crops

As you get to know the plants you are growing, you'll learn to spot their need for watering, feeding, or shading from a hot sun. Pull weeds as they pop up; water before plants look as if they need it; pick or hose off any damaging bugs when you see them. You'll find that this regular attention goes a long way toward eliminating major chores by heading off trouble before it starts.

Watering

Good-tasting vegetables require a steady supply of moisture for uninterrupted growth from seeding to harvest. Too much water will encourage foliage rather than fruit development; too much can also suffocate the roots so they're unable to grow. On the other hand, allowing the roots to dry out will stop growth completely and damage or kill the plant quickly on a hot day. Your watering goal is to keep the moisture level as even as possible, penetrating the soil below root depth and repeating before the soil dries out enough to cause wilting.

How often? Frequency of watering will vary with the weather, your soil, and the size of the plants. Weekly watering might be enough in cool, damp climates, but plants in hot, dry weather demand water at least daily. A sandy soil will need water more frequently than clay soil that drains more slowly. And newly transplanted seedlings will require water more often than well-established crops that need long, deep soaking less frequently.

How much? In an average loam, an inch of water applied at the surface will wet the soil to a depth of 4 to 5 inches (more in sandy soil, less in clay soil). Since even many small vegetables may root to a 12-inch depth, you should apply at least 3 inches of water. Large vegetables feed mainly in the top 12 inches of soil but send out roots to depths of 3 feet or more for anchoring and some water absorption. Apply 6 to 9 inches of water to penetrate to these depths.

If you water in deep furrows between beds, you can roughly measure how much water you apply by gauging the depth of the furrow. When you water with a sprinkler, measure applications in a glass set halfway between the sprinkler and its maximum reach.

Soak. For most gardens, slow soaking of water into the soil is the safest method. It works well for level beds or

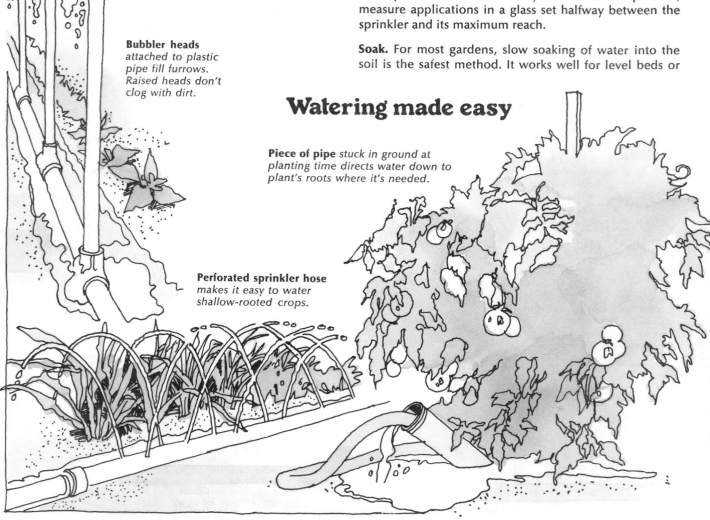

Bubbler heads *attached to plastic pipe fill furrows. Raised heads don't clog with dirt.*

Watering made easy

Piece of pipe *stuck in ground at planting time directs water down to plant's roots where it's needed.*

Perforated sprinkler hose *makes it easy to water shallow-rooted crops.*

terraced slopes and in small gardens where you want to avoid sprinkling certain vegetables.

Except in sandy soils, furrow watering is an efficient method for beds where plants are positioned no more than 3 to 4 inches in from the shoulder of the furrow, since lateral wetting of the soil doesn't go much beyond this. Dig the furrows before planting, making them up to a foot wide and 6 inches deep. Lay them out so they're as level as possible.

Send water into the furrows as slowly as you can so that water can penetrate evenly and soil won't wash away. Penetration will be increased if you divide long furrows into 6-foot segments on sandy soil or 12-foot segments on heavier, less permeable soils. Use a dam made of a board, a piece of metal, or a wide shovel placed upright in the furrow to hold the water until a section of the furrow has been soaked. As the plants grow, move some soil gradually from the sides and bottom of the furrow to the base of the plants to replace any soil that water has eroded away and to help hold plants up.

Watering basins are useful for large, spreading vines, such as cucumbers and melons (see page 15). By confining the water inside the basin and guiding the vines outside it, you will help keep the fruit from rotting on soggy ground.

Sprinkle. Using a good sprinkler that distributes water evenly over the entire surface of the ground is a time-saving way to water a big garden, and many crops thrive under overhead sprinkling.

But overhead watering has some disadvantages, too. Moisture on leaves can encourage rust or mildew in some crops, especially the vine crops such as squash and melon. On very hot days, water on the foliage can cause scalding. Water is also wasted during overhead sprinkling through instant evaporation and splashing. If you do sprinkle, wait until the wind is calm and water in the morning so plants will dry off by evening.

Drip. Systems for applying small, steady amounts of water to a crop are being used by commercial growers to conserve water and save labor but can be adapted to home gardens, especially for large vegetables. In this system, fittings on above-ground plastic hoses drip continuously onto the soil. Look for the type that has grooved plastic attachments without holes that can be clogged. The size of the attachment can be changed, depending on the size of the crop. These systems are distributed through commercial orchard suppliers and many garden supply stores.

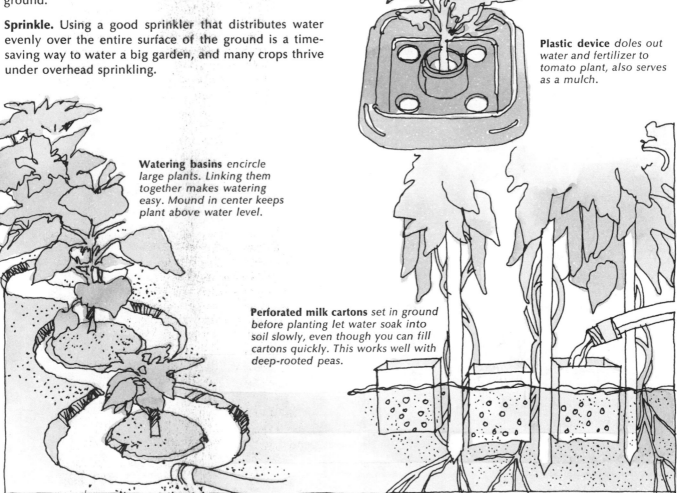

Plastic device doles out water and fertilizer to tomato plant, also serves as a mulch.

Watering basins encircle large plants. Linking them together makes watering easy. Mound in center keeps plant above water level.

Perforated milk cartons set in ground before planting let water soak into soil slowly, even though you can fill cartons quickly. This works well with deep-rooted peas.

Mulching

Covering the soil around your crops with a material called a mulch has these advantages:
- Keeps soil moist by reducing evaporation
- Helps maintain an even soil temperature and warms soil (which encourages early crop maturity)
- Reduces weeds
- Prevents soil crusts from forming (you won't need to cultivate)
- Provides a clean surface for fruit that might rot on wet soil
- Organic mulches add nutrients and humus to the soil as they slowly decompose, keeping the topsoil in prime condition

In case this sounds too good to be true, here are a few pitfalls to watch for: Mulches can be good hiding places for pests such as slugs and sowbugs, so check for these periodically. If you find signs of pests, pull the mulch away from the plants. A mulch spread in the fall can slow down the freezing of winter vegetables, but don't spread a mulch in the spring until the soil has warmed up, or it will keep the soil cold.

Wait until plants have grown past the seedling stage before applying the mulch since a mulch might keep seedlings damp enough to rot. Spread the mulch to cover the soil completely, but leave the stem of the plant exposed where it meets the soil as this part can be susceptible to rot. As the mulch decomposes, reapply it throughout the growing season.

Below are some good mulching materials. Since you will need a lot, choose those that are cheap and abundant in your area.

Tying up

Climbing vegetables such as beans and peas, and sprawling vegetables such as tomatoes, cucumbers, and melons need some help in getting off the ground. Not only will you save space by tying or propping up these crops, but you'll find also that keeping fruit such as tomatoes and pumpkins off the ground will keep them from rotting before they're picked.

Pictured at right are devices you can use for training climbers. Peas and beans can be planted against a garden fence and secured with occasional tying. Sprawling plants need sturdier supports. In very hot climates, don't use metal frames, chicken wire, or galvanized clothesline wire for stringers. Plant leaves and tendrils can burn from touching the hot metal.

Which mulch?

Mulching material	Pros	Cons
Straw or hay	Adds humus as it slowly decomposes.	Can harbor weed seeds and pests. Requires addition of nitrogen to soil.
Peat moss	Improves soil structure.	Expensive. Must be squeezed and kneaded to absorb water before it's applied.
Manure (well-rotted)	Rich in nutrients. Decomposes slowly. Good soil conditioner.	Can burn roots if too fresh. May contain weed seeds.
Leaves (shredded is best; should be at least partially decomposed)	Inexpensive. Readily available.	Requires addition of nitrogen. Unshredded leaves will mat down. May carry weed seeds and pests.
Pine needles	Good source of humus. Decomposes slowly.	Need access to pine trees.
Wood shavings, chips, bark, or sawdust	Inexpensive. Readily available. Clean of weeds and pests. Easy to apply.	Add nitrogen to soil if it hasn't been added to packaged product.
Oats, peanut, buckwheat, or cottonseed hulls	Good humus source. Slow to decompose.	Requires addition of nitrogen. Limited availability.
Newspapers (layer 6–8 sheets thick; cover lightly with soil)	Inexpensive. Readily available.	Add a nitrogen fertilizer before mulching.
Black polyethylene	Weeds can't get through. Most effective soil warmer. Needs infrequent replacement.	May cause excessive heat buildup in hot climates.
Grass clippings	Readily available if you have a lawn.	Spread a thin layer to dry. If applied too thickly they will mat down, become slimy and smelly.

Save space with climbers

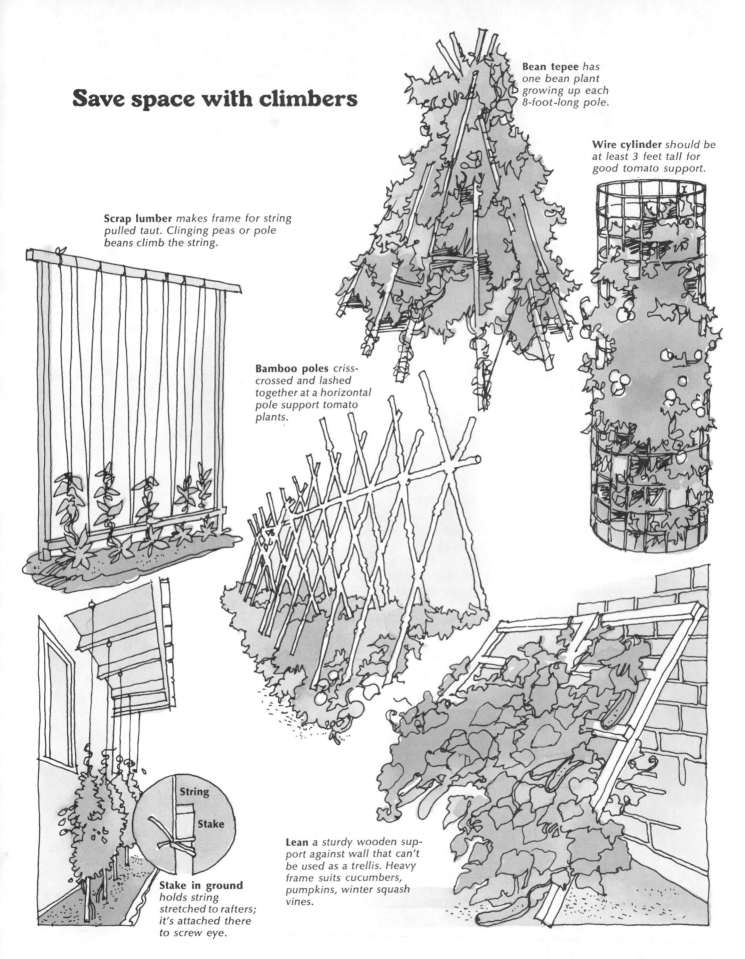

Bean tepee has one bean plant growing up each 8-foot-long pole.

Wire cylinder should be at least 3 feet tall for good tomato support.

Scrap lumber makes frame for string pulled taut. Clinging peas or pole beans climb the string.

Bamboo poles criss-crossed and lashed together at a horizontal pole support tomato plants.

String

Stake

Stake in ground holds string stretched to rafters; it's attached there to screw eye.

Lean a sturdy wooden support against wall that can't be used as a trellis. Heavy frame suits cucumbers, pumpkins, winter squash vines.

Weeding

No one in full command of his senses would probably ever feel that weeding is fun. But it is one of the most important and necessary garden chores since weeds rob surrounding vegetables of food and water and compete with young plants for sunlight.

Hand-pulling, hoeing, and cultivating are all good methods for getting rid of weeds. Hand-pulling and hoeing are best in small gardens; cultivating is more practical in large ones. Avoid cultivating too deeply so you don't disturb feeder roots of vegetables. Dig out deep-rooted weeds with a weeding tool.

Don't use weed-control chemicals near vegetables; they can drift by wind or water and harm your plants.

Here are some labor-saving weeding points:

• Pull weed seedlings as soon as you can distinguish them from the vegetable seedlings.

• Hoe weeds in dry soil to kill roots faster.

• Weeds pulled by hand come out more easily when the soil is moist.

• Never let weeds mature through their growing cycle so they go to seed.

• Gather and compost weeds to keep them from taking root in the garden again after being pulled up.

If you have trouble

Pests and diseases particularly bothersome to each vegetable are listed in the Gardener's Guide. Use the methods described there if pests begin to do actual damage. Following are general precautions you can take to discourage damage to your crops:

• Plant disease-resistant varieties if available. Resistant hybrids have been developed for the most troublesome vegetable diseases. Many excellent tomato hybrids, for example, are resistant to verticillium and fusarium wilt.

• Encourage healthy plant growth by providing optimum growing conditions. Rich, well-drained soil will support the kind of healthy plant that is less susceptible to attacks of insects or diseases.

• Keep your garden tidy. Clean up debris that can become breeding and hiding places for harmful creatures. Inspect mulch for signs of insects and pull the mulch away from a plant if you see any signs of trouble.

• Don't concentrate crops in just one place. Large expanses of one type of plant encourage pests that thrive on that plant. Mixed plantings confuse insects' sense of smell, making it harder for them to locate the crops they feed on. Mixed plantings also can sustain a greater array of friendly insects (parasites and predators of the bad guys).

• Look carefully; then leap. While you're watering, weeding, and harvesting your crops, keep a watchful eye out for the first signs of damage. If you see a big troublemaker in action, pick it off and destroy it. Wash small insects off with a strong jet of water from the hose. If the damage is being done by such night creatures as snails, slugs, and cutworms, you will have to look for them at night with a flashlight or trap them under boards or in sheets of rolled-up newspapers where they will hide during the day.

• Encourage natural controls. Many birds, toads, and lizards eat insects. You can buy some beneficial insects from mail-order sources (ladybugs, praying mantises, lacewings, and trichogramma wasps). Don't depend on these insects to wipe out your entire pest population — it's possible that they'll fly over the fence at the first opportunity. If you have a wide variety of pests for them to feed on, though, these good insects may colonize and cut down considerably on crop damage. Ladybugs, lacewings, and praying mantises concentrate on aphids and other soft-bodied insects. Trichogramma wasps destroy moth eggs before they hatch into cabbage loopers and other leaf-eating caterpillars.

• Aromatic plants, such as garlic, onions, hot peppers, and marigolds, may ward off some pests with their strong odors. Plant them around the vegetables that seem most susceptible to damage.

• Spray or dust only as a last resort. You should use sprays only if a specific pest gets out of hand on a particular crop. Slight damage to crops is not the signal to start a chemical war. Learn to accept a few holes in the lettuce or a few plants lost to the troublemakers.

Homemade sprays. Some gardeners have found that a soap mixture sprayed on the plant will destroy mealybugs and aphids. Mix 9 level tablespoons of old-fashioned soap flakes, not detergent, in 3 gallons of water.

You can try discouraging other insects by grinding strong-smelling plants such as hot peppers, onions, garlic, or marigolds and blending with an equal amount of water. Strain out the liquid and use 1 teaspoon of the liquid extract to a pint of water.

Botanical sprays. Rotenone, pyrethrum, and ryania are toxic to insects but relatively safe to man. Because they have little residual effect, you must apply them directly to the insect. They control some of the common sucking and chewing insects, such as beetles, whiteflies, and aphids.

Manufactured chemicals. Only three manufactured insecticides on the market should be used by home gardeners on vegetables: diazinon, malathion, and sevin. (Sevin, however, kills honeybees.) These should be applied strictly according to label directions. They are most effective against sucking insects such as aphids, thrips, leaf hoppers, and whiteflies. Many sprays for vegetables contain a mixture of these chemicals — check the label to be sure that the formulation you use is certified for edible crops. *Never* use any spray that isn't specifically recommended on the label for vegetables. Follow the directions *exactly* as to how long before harvest you must spray.

Biological controls. Certain bacterial cultures can kill specific insects without harm to warm-blooded creatures. Several manufacturers offer products containing *Bacillus thuringiensis*, which can control several insects in their caterpillar stage. "Milky spore disease" spores are available for control of Japanese beetles.

Now, about those pests...

Use this page to identify the most common vegetable pests. (Consult your county farm advisor about local pest problems.) Once you know what's doing the damage, check the listing for a particular vegetable in the Gardener's Guide to learn any special considerations for dealing with pests that plant may attract. If you have tried removing the pest by hand or by hose and it continues to do serious damage to the crop, spray only with a product that specifies on its label that it can be used for vegetables. Allow the recommended time before harvest.

If you find holes in your leaves . . .

Snails and slugs

Find them eating at night and on overcast days and pick them off. Sprinkle ashes around plants. Set out boards; check during the day. Use snail bait.

Bean beetles

Pick them off of foliage. Some of them feed at night—look for them by flashlight. Use rotenone, malathion, sevin, ryania, or diazinon.

Cucumber beetles

Find these on squash and melons as well as cucumbers and pick them off. Use rotenone, malathion, sevin, or diazinon.

Cabbage worms

Hand pick them from cabbage, broccoli, Brussels sprouts, cauliflower. Use Bacillus thuringiensis, rotenone, or malathion before heads form.

If tiny bugs suck plant juices . . .

Aphids

These can be green, black, yellow, or pink. Hose off with water or soap solution. Use rotenone, malathion, ryania, pyrethrum, or sevin.

Leafhoppers

Fast-moving green or brownish bugs feed on underside of leaf, causing white stippling on top. Common on beans. Use malathion or sevin.

Spider mites

Finely stippled leaves with silvery webs on underside; you need a hand lens to see the mites. Wash them off. Use malathion or diazinon.

Whiteflies

Look for them on the underside of leaves, especially on beans and tomatoes. Hose off with water or soap solution. Use malathion or rotenone.

If borers eat into leaves and fruit . . .

Leaf miners

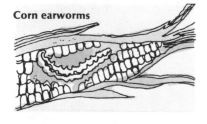

Insects lay eggs on leaf surface. Larvae enter leaves; feeding results in a serpentine trail. Pick off infested leaves. Use rotenone.

Corn earworms

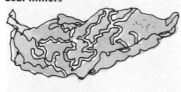

These crawl into the ear of corn. Cut silks 3 days after ears reach full size. Put mineral oil on silks (see page 49). Use ryania.

If you discover burrowers in the soil . . .

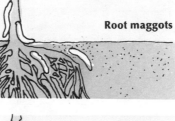

Root maggots

Commonly found on the cabbage family and root crops. Use a tarpaper collar (see page 17). Use diazinon around seedlings.

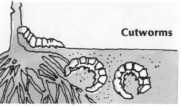

Cutworms

These moth caterpillars cut off stems at ground level or eat leaves. Use a tarpaper collar. Use sevin or diazinon.

Harvesting and storing your crops

Follow the recommendations under each vegetable in the Gardener's Guide for harvesting each at its peak of tenderness and sweetness. If you wait beyond this point, the sugar of peas and corn will turn to starch, beans will become stringy, and beets woody. If possible, harvest early in the morning when the sugar content is highest. Before harvesting root crops, water the soil first so roots will come up without breaking.

For most vegetables, picking and tasting a few is the only sure test of readiness. Harvesting a crop too early not only prevents it from reaching full size but also often detracts from its developing full flavor. Harvesting too late may increase crop size but often at the expense of tenderness. Also, a vegetable left on the plant too long drains plant energy, causing a slowdown in production.

In cold-winter areas before severe frosts, you can prepare root crops, such as carrots, beets, turnips, rutabagas, and parsnips, for winter storage by digging the roots and removing the leaves. Dig cabbage, Brussels sprouts, and Chinese cabbage (roots and all) when the foliage is dry. Wet foliage can cause the whole pile to rot. Knock the soil off the roots; remove the outer leaves. Don't wash vegetables before storing them. Make a 6-inch layer of dry leaves or hay; lay the vegetables on it in a shallow layer. Mound leaves or hay 12 to 24 inches deep over the vegetables, covering them with a plastic sheet held down with soil. This insulation should prevent the vegetables from freezing until extremely cold weather arrives. Some gardeners utilize coldframes as root cellars for fall storage of heading or rooting vegetables, filling them with leaves as insulation.

Another means of storing vegetables in cold-winter areas is in a trash can sunk in the ground. This modified root cellar works particularly well with root crops. Dig a hole deep enough that you can recess the can to within 3 to 4 inches of the rim. Use moist sand at the bottom of the can and between layers of vegetables to prevent drying out. A plastic-covered straw or leaf mulch over the can cover will provide additional insulation.

Those vegetables requiring cool, dry storage conditions (see list on opposite page) can be kept in a well-ventilated cellar away from a heat source. For good air circulation, store in containers such as slatted boxes. Onions store well when hung in mesh bags or old nylons.

Keep out the creatures

If your garden has become a salad bar for rabbits, gophers, or deer, the most effective solution is to fence them out. Raised beds lined on the bottom with ½-inch hardware cloth or aviary wire will keep such burrowers as gophers or moles away from succulent roots (see pages 10–11).

A rabbit-proof fence should be at least 2 feet tall and go at least 6 inches underground. Rabbits can burrow under that, but you should be able to notice the holes before they get all the way under.

A deerproof fence should be at least 8 feet high. If your building code doesn't allow this, use an outrigger structure to discourage deer — they don't like to jump very far.

If you live in an area where you have many of these persistent visitors, a cage might be the answer to keeping all of them away, including birds. As a bonus, the cage can be covered with a sheet or other material to protect winter crops from frosty nights and cool-season crops from hot weather.

Portable cage covered with chicken wire keeps nibblers away from tasty seedlings.

Discourage burrowing animals by folding out bottom foot of wire and staking it down.

After they're picked

To take full advantage of the fresh flavor you can't buy in a store, use most of the vegetables you grow immediately after picking. If you have a surplus, though, you'll want to check the lists below — they show which vegetables can be canned, dried, frozen, or kept in cold storage. The *Sunset* book *Home Canning* gives detailed instructions.

Keep unwashed in refrigerator	Use as soon as possible	To preserve
Artichokes	''	Freeze whole; can, dry, or freeze hearts
Asparagus	''	Can, dry, or freeze
Broccoli	''	Dry or freeze
Corn	''	Can, dry, or freeze
Cucumbers	''	Freeze, puree, or pickle
Eggplant	''	Dry or freeze
Endive	''	Use fresh
Lettuce	''	Use fresh
Mustard greens	''	Use fresh
Peas	''	Can, dry, or freeze
Radishes	''	Use fresh
Spinach	''	Dry or freeze
Tomatoes	''	Can, dry, or freeze

Store in cold, moist pit or root cellar	Length of storage	To preserve
Beets	3–10 weeks	Can, dry, or freeze
Brussels sprouts	3–4 weeks	Dry or freeze
Cabbage	12–16 weeks	Dry or freeze
Carrots	16–20 weeks	Can, dry, or freeze
Cauliflower	2–3 weeks	Pickle, dry, or freeze
Celery	8–16 weeks	Can, dry, or freeze
Kohlrabi	2–4 weeks	Use fresh
Leeks	4–12 weeks	Use fresh
Melons	2–4 weeks	Freeze
Onions, green	4–12 weeks	Use fresh
Parsnips	8–16 weeks	Freeze
Peppers	4–6 weeks	Can, dry, or freeze
Potatoes	12–20 weeks	Can, dry, or freeze
Rhubarb	2–3 weeks	Can or freeze
Rutabagas	8–16 weeks	Freeze
Squash, summer	2–3 weeks	Can, dry, or freeze
Turnips	8–12 weeks	Can

Keep cool and dry	Length of storage	To preserve
Garlic	24–32 weeks	Use fresh
Onions, bulbing	12–32 weeks	Can, dry, or freeze
Pumpkins	8–24 weeks	Can, dry, or freeze
Squash, winter	8–24 weeks	Can, dry, or freeze

Vegetable Ingenuity ...a Potpourri of Ideas

What if you don't have a flat spot of land in the sun? Use this section and your imagination to help you grow vegetables anyway. If your apartment balcony faces south or west, try hanging baskets. If you live on a hillside, terrace the slope. Containers can go anywhere — even move with you. If none of these fit your style, get together with your neighbors and start a community garden on a vacant lot. In fact, even if you have a big, sunny backyard, some of these approaches might be fun to try.

Start a community garden

A community garden can be as simple as a group of neighbors banding together to plant vegetables on a vacant lot or as elaborate as a city-owned, city-run project where you rent a plot for a nominal fee. Ideal for people who live in city apartments or whose homes lack backyard growing space, these gardens also can save participants money through such shared items as tools and amendments bought in quantity.

Your first step is to find out if a garden that you can join has already been organized in your area. If not, informally survey your neighbors to find out how many are seriously interested in such a project. Even if you take on the job of coordinator, you'll want to spread jobs around to people willing to help organize. Here are some considerations:

Land. Scout your area for vacant land that gets sun all day, provides enough room for your group (figure about 15 by 25 feet per household plus ample path space), and ideally has a convenient source of water (installing water lines can be expensive). Your assessor's office can help you find the owner of a likely lot.

Inventive use of idle — and sometimes unsightly — land has become a big bonus of the community garden movement. Seldom-used parks, church and school grounds, excess commercial or government acreage, urban renewal land, and company land (for employee

groups) have been favorite sites. Rights-of-way under power lines and along flood channels and abandoned rail lines are likely sites, but consider other alternatives before you garden near or under a pollution-laden freeway. Avoid leases that can be canceled before harvest.

City help. Find out if your city will help by providing land, water installation, or clearing of debris. Try the park or recreation department in your city to find out if it has undertaken any similar projects.

Improving soil. Bulk rates on quantities of amendments are an advantage of a shared garden. Try farms and dairies, park maintenance agencies, and stables. See the section on raised beds and double digging, pages 10–11, for effective methods of improving poor soil.

Formalities. Insurance protects the property owner and you from injury and damage arising from gardening activity. Cities that sponsor community gardens often add them to their existing policies; otherwise check with your insurance company about a group policy.

You'll probably want some kind of fence at least to keep stray dogs out of the plots. A combination lock will insure that the melons you've been nurturing will be there when you're ready to pick them. You'll also want to decide on a place to keep tools — one that is secure but accessible.

If your land isn't level

If you have a scarcity of level land for growing vegetables, don't despair. It takes a bit more work to prevent soil erosion and keep the water from running downhill, but you can grow vegetables on a slope.

For a gentle slope, run the rows on the contour lines of the hill — rows running up and down the hill are difficult to irrigate.

On a steeper slope, terracing is the ideal solution. When you remove the topsoil to create the terraces, set it aside and return it when the terraces are level. Provide a slight slope on each terrace along the contour line to prevent standing water. Retaining walls of wood or stone make the beds permanent. On heavy soils, lay drainage lines or use gravel fill behind the walls to prevent bulging or collapse from water pressure.

If you just want to plant a few vegetables on sloping land and don't want to undertake a terracing project, try the watering ideas on pages 18 and 19. Sunken, perforated milk cartons or other bottomless containers are particularly good for soaking hillside vegetables without water running downhill.

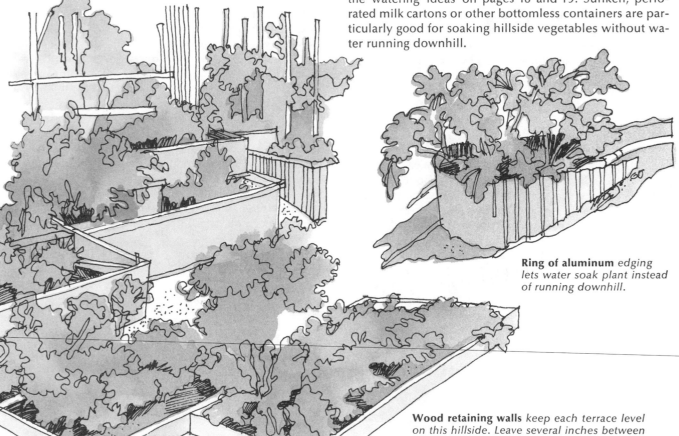

Ring of aluminum *edging lets water soak plant instead of running downhill.*

Wood retaining walls *keep each terrace level on this hillside. Leave several inches between soil and top of board for watering.*

Vegetables in the greenhouse

If you have a greenhouse, you can grow a few containers of vegetables in it the year around, or you can give over the entire space to a vegetable garden. The vegetables you can grow depend on whether your greenhouse is heated or unheated. Cool-weather crops such as lettuce, carrots, and celery thrive in an unheated greenhouse; tomatoes, cucumbers, and peppers need more warmth.

Vegetables require a lot of space, so look for dwarf varieties and climbers that can be trained up supports. Hanging baskets save space, too (see next page). If you've decided to give edible crops more space than a few containers, consider building raised beds on the floor of the greenhouse (see page 11).

Vegetables that flower will probably require hand pollination since insects won't be around to do the job. Do this in one of three ways:

• Use a soft camel's hair brush on each of the blossom clusters to move the pollen from flower to flower.
• Gently shake the plant.
• If your greenhouse has a fan for ventilation, this should circulate the pollen. You could also bring in a portable fan during flowering time and let it run for a few days.

Container crops

If you are short on tillable ground, you might try growing vegetables in containers. Large wooden boxes, barrels cut in half, pressed pulp tubs, and large clay pots all make practical containers deep enough for all but the very largest vegetables. Besides not allowing enough root room, containers that are too small dry out too fast and are easily tipped over. If a container doesn't have drainage holes, drill them into the bottom and cover them with pieces of clay pot or rock so the soil doesn't run out with the water.

For hanging baskets, choose a clay pot or wooden box with holes in the rim or line a wire basket with moss and then fill with soil. (A 12-inch container is a good size for most vegetables.) Since the container will be very heavy when wet and loaded with mature plants, use big hooks for hanging them and double up on the wire supports. When you hang the basket, check that the bottom is high enough to avoid heads (about 7 feet).

Fill the containers with a porous, fast-draining soil mix. A heavy soil does not absorb water readily enough or drain fast enough to promote good root formation. A heavy soil mass will also tend to shrink away from the sides of the containers so that water will pour down the sides of the dry root ball rather than penetrating it. Use a commercial mix or make your own with one part garden loam, one part river sand, and one part leaf mold or peat moss.

If you use an artificial soil, such as U.C. mix, add lime and superphosphate to correct acidity and guarantee that sufficient phosphorus will be immediately available to the roots. (Add 5 to 8 pounds dolomitic limestone and 2 to 3 pounds superphosphate per cubic yard of soil.) Incorporating up to one-quarter soil into the mix will supply micronutrients not contained in the other ingredients and will add beneficial soil organisms.

To maintain steady growth, feed vegetables weekly with a fertilizer such as fish emulsion, diluted as directed on the label, or use a controlled-release fertilizer that provides the nutrients for the entire growing season from a single application. Check the soil for moisture daily — containers will probably need watering at least that often in hot weather.

Check the Gardener's Guide, pages 34-75, to find if a vegetable you want to grow would be successful in containers. Consider, too, the following points when deciding which crops to grow:

• If the containers will be on display, the plants should be attractive, even during harvest. Fruiting plants, such as tomatoes, peppers, and eggplant, fall into this category, as well as such plants as Swiss chard that continue to grow even though outer leaves are harvested.

• Select crops — such as radishes, lettuce, and chives — that grow quickly so you can harvest them and replant another crop in the same container.

• Choose vegetables that yield a satisfying harvest from one or two plants. It would be impractical to use a number of containers for just one meal.

• Cherry tomatoes, cucumbers, eggplant, and New Zealand spinach make prime candidates for hanging baskets.

Seven container ideas

Half-barrels *are often the largest of the reasonably priced, attractive containers available.*

Paper pulp *pots made from recycled paper last about 3 years, longer if you keep them on surfaces other than soil.*

1 x 10s

1 x 2s

To make planting box *shown, cut 1 by 10 boards to desired length and width. Nail end pieces inside long boards. Then nail bottom pieces to frame, setting all but end pieces slightly apart for drainage. Base strips made of 1 by 2s keep box off ground. To keep soil from sifting out, line bottom of box with two layers of newspaper punched with holes.*

Tools you will need

You can prepare a planting bed and tend your vegetables with the basic tools that have been used for centuries: a shovel, rake, hoe, trowel, and weeding tool. You'll see a wide range of styles and prices, but look for well-built tools that fit your hands. For preparing beds, a round-pointed shovel will take care of most of the digging and amendment-moving jobs. A good, all-purpose hoe is the chopper type, which will work for making furrows as well as for weeding.

If you make compost, you'll need a spading fork to turn the pile. A machete will come in handy, too, for chopping heavy stalks into small bits before you compost them. In areas where the soil is hard, you may need a pickax to break it up.

A wheel cultivator can take the place of some of these tools and is useful in a large vegetable garden that is planted in rows. Attachments serve to cut weed roots, loosen the soil, and form furrows, although the soil must be loosened initially by spading or rototilling.

For very large gardens, power equipment, such as a rototiller for breaking up earth or a shredder-grinder for making compost, can save a great deal of work. You may want to rent, rather than buy, expensive equipment that you use infrequently. Renting before you buy will also help you decide whether or not to make the investment.

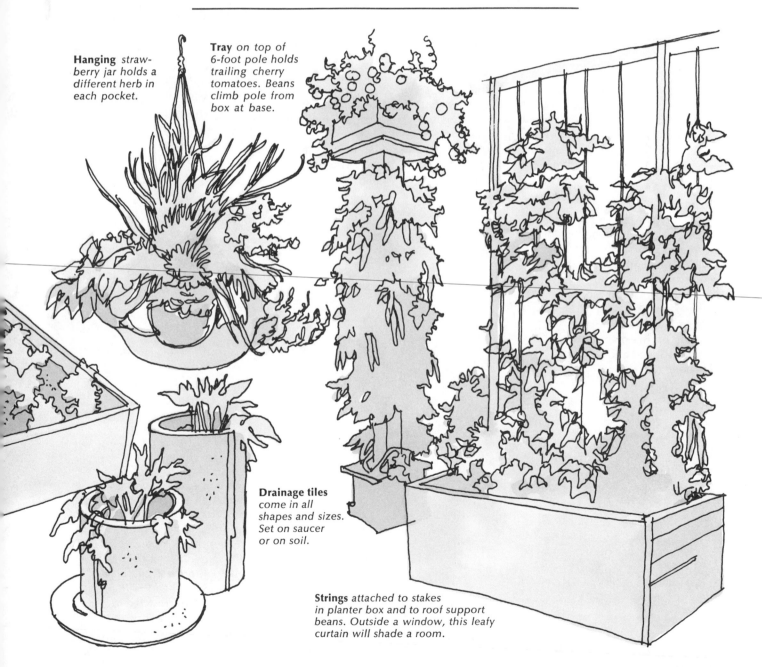

Hanging *strawberry jar holds a different herb in each pocket.*

Tray *on top of 6-foot pole holds trailing cherry tomatoes. Beans climb pole from box at base.*

Drainage tiles *come in all shapes and sizes. Set on saucer or on soil.*

Strings *attached to stakes in planter box and to roof support beans. Outside a window, this leafy curtain will shade a room.*

Vegetables out of the ordinary

Vegetable gourd. Both ornamental and edible, this gourd can be sown, cared for, and cooked like winter squash. Gourds measure about 4 inches across; their flesh is a creamy white. Vines grow vigorously and bear fruit abundantly.

Celtuce. A dual-purpose vegetable from China, celtuce provides leaves to use like lettuce and stalks to use like celery. Harvest leaves when they are young and tender; when the leaves start getting tough, stop harvesting them and let the stalk fatten up (from ¾ to 3 inches in diameter). Then pull up roots and all and use as you would celery, removing tough leaves.

Arugula. Also called roquette, this Italian salad green has a spicy tang something like cress or horseradish. Sow seed as you would sow lettuce — it should sprout in 3 or 4 days. Harvest tender young leaves without pulling up the plant until it goes to seed and leaves become bitter.

Sorrel. A staple in French and eastern European cuisines, sorrel tastes like tangy spinach and can be used raw or cooked like spinach. Plant seeds or nursery plants in early spring and harvest by pulling leaves from the plant, always leaving a few to keep the plant nourished. This perennial will continue to produce all year in mild winters and go dormant where the ground freezes, reviving earlier than other vegetables. If plants become crowded in 2 or 3 years, dig and divide in spring, replanting the divisions in enriched soil.

Chayote. This perennial member of the squash family can be eaten raw or cooked like squash. It's from the tropics and strictly a plant for mild-winter climates — cold weather slows growth and production and frost kills plants completely. In mild winters, the tops of the tall vines will die back, but the roots send up new growth each spring for many years.

Plant at least two whole fruits (for cross-pollination) with the large end down and the small end exposed. Buy the fruit in the winter and store in a cool place (the refrigerator is too cold) until the soil warms up in the spring.

Be careful not to overwater at first; overwatering causes the fruit to rot. Once the vine starts to grow, it needs occasional fertilizing and ample water. Plants begin to bloom around the end of August; fruits come about a month later. In warm weather, plants may bear through December and January and produce as many as 50 to 100 fruits to the vine.

Fennel. Grow your own breath freshener! Fennel seeds have a mild, sweet licorice flavor that freshens your breath when you chew it. But this tall, weedy-looking plant has other uses as well. Flavor fish, salads, and vegetables with its feathery leaves or with the seeds; or use the globe at the base of the stalk as you'd use celery (the kind with the edible stem is *Foeniculum vulgare dulce*, sometimes called finocchio).

Sow seeds in early spring and again in summer for fall crop. If you don't want the plants to take over your garden, dig out the large tap root so new shoots keep coming, and harvest seeds before they scatter to prevent self-sowing.

Sponge gourd or loofa sponge. You can eat this gourd or let it mature on the vine and use it as a sponge. The fruit's flavor is a cross between cucumber and summer squash and the flesh can be used raw or cooked.

To eat, harvest before the seeds develop (about 90 days) when the gourds are between 6 and 12 inches long. Once gourds mature, the plant stops producing. As gourds overmature, their ridges turn brown and the flesh toughens into a spongy cylinder. To use gourds as sponges, leave them on the vine until they're all brown; then pick and dry completely. Crush the skin lightly and soak in boiling water until it's soft enough to peel off easily. Soak in bleach if the fiber is discolored.

Sprouts to eat

Neither insects nor the weather can affect the sprouts you grow in your kitchen, and you'll be eating the results within days instead of weeks or months.

There are two types of sprouts. The tiny ones that you eat when they form green leaves are alfalfa, cress, chia, mustard, and radish. The larger ones that you eat before the leaves open or turn green are fenugreek, lentils, mung beans (the kind you see in the grocery store), wheat, and rye. You use the same method to sprout both kinds.

First, soak the seeds in water until they are saturated— a few hours for the small ones, overnight for the large ones. Use a colander (not a metal one) for the larger sprouts; sprinkle smaller sprouts on damp cheesecloth spread in a shallow dish (not metal). A glass jar with cheesecloth or screen fitted under the jar ring works well, too. Keep it on its side in filtered light.

Rinse or spray the seeds with lukewarm water several times a day. The object is to keep them moist (but not wet) and fairly warm (at least 68°F.).

When the seeds sprout, give them plenty of light, except for mung beans and fenugreek, which should be kept in the dark until ready for use. Use sprouts with or without the seed hulls in cooked dishes or raw in sandwiches or salads.

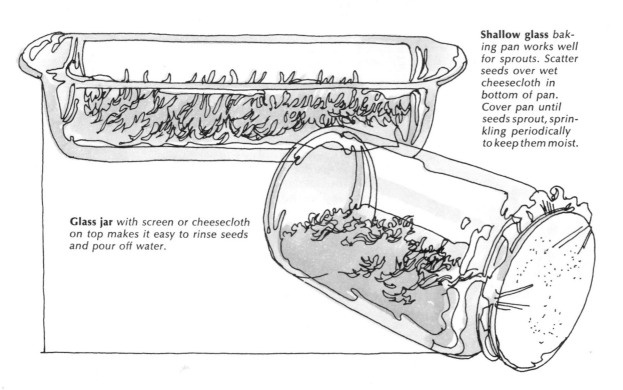

Shallow glass *baking pan works well for sprouts. Scatter seeds over wet cheesecloth in bottom of pan. Cover pan until seeds sprout, sprinkling periodically to keep them moist.*

Glass jar *with screen or cheesecloth on top makes it easy to rinse seeds and pour off water.*

The edible landscape

More and more homeowners are digging up front lawns and replacing them with vegetable gardens, but if you want to be more subtle about working them into the landscape, try the ideas listed below. The secret of success is treating crops as ornamentals by planting them in clumps instead of rows. Planting seeds indoors and having them ready for succession planting also helps by minimizing bare spots between crops.

* Try lettuce or parsley to border a flower bed.
* Dig up a circle in the middle of a lawn and grow salad greens in concentric circles — for example, a circle of green lettuce on the outside, then a circle of parsley, a circle of red lettuce, and in the center carrots and radishes.

* Plant bush squash or eggplant next to a patio.
* Line a walkway with peppers or Swiss chard.
* Mix small vegetables in between newly planted annuals to provide foliage in the bare spots. By the time you harvest the carrots, lettuce, or parsley, the annuals will have spread out to fill the space.
* In seed catalogs and racks, look for colorful vegetable varieties such as 'Golden Egg', a white, round eggplant; 'Rhubarb', a Swiss chard with crimson stalks and veins; 'Royalty', a purple pod bush bean; and any of the red and yellow peppers.
* In mild-winter climates, artichokes make a year-round show, especially if you leave some of the 'chokes on the bush so the flowers will turn purple.

An experiment in hydroponics

Hydroponics means "working water," and, although you can choose among many methods, all of them work on the same principle: the plant receives all of its nutrients from the watering solution instead of from the soil.

To try this yourself, start several seeds with any of the methods described on pages 12-15. When secondary leaves appear on the seedlings, transplant each into a pot filled with lightweight gravel to one inch of the top. The container should have a cork or stopper for the drainage hole. Mix a commercial hydroponic plant food according to directions on the package, making enough solution to fill the container to the top of the gravel.

Twice a day, water the plant with the solution, leaving the plug in the drainage hole until the container is full. Then pull the plug, catching the excess in a bucket or pan to use for the next feeding. Repeat this schedule for a week; then mix up a new batch and continue to feed twice a day. The plant food supplies all the nutrients that the plant needs to grow and produce fruit.

Other methods use planting mediums that are more conventional. For an indoor container, try half peat moss and half vermiculite as a planting mix. Feed each plant 8 ounces of nutrient solution every other day.

Outdoors fill a raised bed or planter box with 1 part sand and 3 parts sawdust. Feed each plant 8 ounces of nutrient solution once a week and water twice a week with plain water (three times a week in hot weather).

Once you succeed with a plant grown hydroponically, you might want to try one of the devices available that make the feeding automatic. These range from single containers to greenhouse units with pump, timers, and hoses — the ultimate in hydroponics. With these, you can plant a cherry tomato seedling and not touch it again until the tomatoes are ready.

Sensor

Water

Soil

Water feed valve

Top: *Automatic watering and feeding device keeps moisture and nutrients at correct level for healthy growth.*

Left: *Nutrient solution drains out of planter through hose, back into bucket where it's ready for recycling.*

A Gardener's Guide to Vegetables

In this guide you will discover answers to such questions as which vegetables are the easiest to grow and which are the most difficult, which will deliver the fastest harvest and which the slowest, which are practically free of problems and which almost ask for trouble.

For quick reference, the major kinds of vegetables are listed in alphabetical order. Under each heading you will find recommendations for the best varieties to choose and specific directions for planting, watering, feeding, dealing with pests, harvesting, and container use.

Artichokes

Large, bushy perennial. Set out root divisions in early spring; harvest 'chokes the following spring.

Long, mild winters and cool summers are needed to produce the heavy vegetative growth that supports the large, edible flower buds of this delicacy. Highly decorative, massive plants have huge, deeply cut leaves. These well up into a silvery green fountain that can spread to 6 feet wide. Flower buds that escape harvest ripen into large, violet pink thistle blossoms that can be dried for arrangements and will last for several years. Three or four established plants will provide plenty of artichoke buds for a small family.

Recommended variety. 'Green Globe' is usually the only variety available.

How to plant. You can grow artichokes from root divisions either purchased or separated from a desirable mother plant. Divide roots in autumn when foliage has died back. Expose a side shoot with a sharp spray of water. Cut it off 6 to 8 inches below the crown. Rangy plants with small, late-maturing buds may result if you start from seeds.

In early spring, root divisions are available in nurseries or garden supply stores and by mail order. In the West and along the Gulf and Southeastern coasts, you can plant the divisions any time after late winter.

Choose a spot that has well-drained, fertile soil and is warmed by full sun, except in very hot areas where artichokes appreciate afternoon shade. For root divisions, dig holes that are 18 inches deep, 4 to 5 feet apart. Fill the hole with water and let it soak in. For each plant, mix a bucketful of organic matter with some of the removed soil and partially refill the holes. Position the roots vertically, covering the old root with soil but leaving the base of the new, leafy shoots just above the soil line. Water again to settle the soil and complete filling the hole. Water every other day until new growth appears.

Care. Pull or hoe weeds or spread a straw mulch under the leaf canopy. Weeds steal water and nutrients from the plants. Every week or two during dry weather, let the hose trickle for an hour or two at the base of the plants.

Artichokes are heavy feeders and will respond to high nitrogen, water-soluble fertilizers applied every three to four weeks. Feed after a heavy watering. Follow the feeding with a light watering to dissolve and flush the fertilizer down into the root zone.

Pests. Aphids, earwigs, and worms sometimes get between the leaf bracts in the artichokes. If you think this has happened, right after picking immerse the artichokes for 10 minutes in warm salt water. The critters will crawl out. Give the buds a final upside-down shaking to force out the stubborn ones.

Harvesting. Each plant should bear a few buds the first season. From the second year on, plants should produce from 24 to 48 buds from late winter through midsummer. The harvest period will be earlier where winters are warm.

Cut the buds before the fleshy, edible bracts begin to open in preparation for flowering. Leave a 1½-inch length of stem on each bud when you cut it. After each major stem has completed fruiting, it will begin to dry up and can be removed. New, fruiting shoots will form throughout the season.

In containers. These handsome plants will thrive in containers with a soil capacity of at least 2 cubic feet.

Asparagus

One of the earliest vegetable crops. Set out roots as early in the year as they're available. Wait two years for the first harvest.

The tasty spears of this hardy perennial push up from heavy root masses from early spring until warm weather arrives and occasionally through midsummer. (Asparagus needs a winter dormancy period to thrive.) Mature asparagus plants look completely unlike the spears; they reach from 4 to 6 feet in height and billow out to a width of 3 feet. These feathery, decorative plumes should be left on the plant until they have begun to dry in late autumn; they manufacture the food reserves that maintain strong crowns from year to year. Cut the stems to the ground only after foliage turns brown.

Although asparagus takes several years to come into full production, the plants are very long lived — up to 20 years or more. Two dozen plants should yield enough spears for a small family.

Recommended varieties. Avoid problems with rust disease by planting resistant varieties such as 'California 500', 'Mary Washington', 'Waltham Washington'. 'U.C. 711' is another recommended variety.

How to plant. Since three years are required to produce spears from seed-grown plants, most gardeners prefer to start from roots. Roots are available during the late winter in Western states and can be planted as early as they are available. In other areas, mail order is the usual source. Plant the roots as soon as you receive them.

Asparagus plants need lots of room and full sun. Plant them at the back of the garden or along a fence where the tall foliage won't be in the way. Because the plants will be in place for many years, the soil should be broken up to a depth of 18 inches and large volumes of organic matter, such as well-rotted manure, should be worked in thoroughly. Don't skimp on the width of the bed; the prepared soil should extend 18 inches beyond the crowns. Mixing in organic matter should raise the bed 2 to 3 inches above surrounding soil; this improves drainage.

To plant the roots, dig trenches 12 inches deep and 12 to 18 inches wide; trenches should be spaced 4 feet apart. Place 2 to 3 inches of manure in each trench, and sprinkle a complete fertilizer (5-10-10 formula) over the manure (use 1½ to 2 pounds fertilizer for each 25 feet of trench). Mix together the manure, fertilizer, and some soil, then add several inches of soil to protect the roots from the manure. Mound the soil toward the center of the trench; the top of the mound should be about 6 inches below garden level. Place root crowns 12 to 18 inches apart on top of the mound, so roots can spread downward. Cover the roots with 2 inches of soil and water thoroughly. As stalks appear, gradually fill in the trench.

Care. Cultivate only in the top inch of the soil so you don't injure the network of roots. Pull weeds by hand before they get started in the bed, where they will be difficult to pull out without injuring the asparagus roots.

Perforated sprinkler hoses provide an excellent device for the deep watering needed by asparagus, since beds are too wide for basins or furrows. Let the sprinkler run for several hours every week or two during dry weather.

Feed with a complete fertilizer high in nitrogen when plants put on a growth spurt — usually around midsummer. When you remove the brown foliage in the fall, add a mulch of 2 to 3 inches of coarse organic matter such as well-rotted manure. Do not use peat moss or leaves as a mulch; they form a crust or pack down, preventing moisture from penetrating the bed and hindering emerging spears.

Pests. The organic mulch over the beds makes a good hiding place for snails, slugs, sowbugs, and earwigs. Scatter meal or pellets of bait over the bed every two to three weeks to control them. Control asparagus beetles with sevin, malathion, or rotenone after the cutting period (follow label precautions). Don't spray after spears have poked their heads up, since they grow rapidly and will be cut within days.

Harvesting. Begin harvesting spears the second year after planting crowns or the third year after planting seeds. Harvest for two to three weeks or until the spears start appearing thinner. Then let them grow foliage for the rest of the season.

Cut spears when they are 6 to 8 inches high, at a point between the surface of the soil and 1½ inches deep, trying to avoid injury to the crowns or spears developing below the surface.

At the start of the cutting season, you will probably be able to harvest some spears every three days. As the soil warms, you may have to harvest daily. Spears taller than 8 inches have passed the best harvest stage, so let them develop foliage.

In containers. A wide-spreading root system makes asparagus a poor choice for container growing.

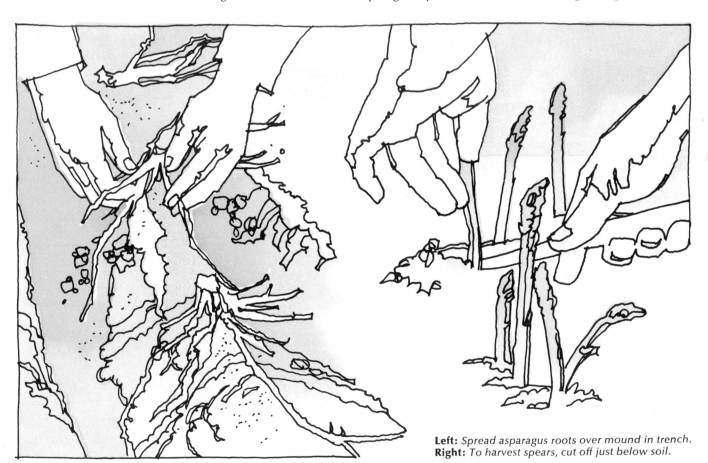

Left: *Spread asparagus roots over mound in trench.*
Right: *To harvest spears, cut off just below soil.*

Beans

When the weather warms, beans will go from seed to table in 60 days. The biggest problem is deciding which of the many kinds to grow.

Left to right: *lima, snap, yardlong, purple pod, yellow wax, soy*

The two types of beans most frequently grown by home gardeners are snap beans and lima beans. Each of these can be divided into two kinds: low growing (bush beans) and tall growing (pole or runner beans). The legume family also contains many delicious vegetables that have beanlike seeds but that only remotely resemble the familiar types of beans. These include fava or broad beans, Southern peas, and asparagus, or yardlong, beans. The similarities in the culture of all of these beans are discussed first; then their individual characteristics are noted.

How to plant. Plant beans from seeds sown in the ground as soon as the soil has warmed up. Beans are frost tender and require a soil temperature of 65° to sprout reliably. Either check the soil temperature with a soil thermometer or wait until late-leafing trees — oaks, hickories, pecans — uncurl new spring foliage. Successive crops may be planted until midsummer.

Plant seeds of bush beans 3 inches apart in rows 18 to 24 inches apart. Pole bean plants are much larger, requiring 3 feet between rows and 6 to 12 inches between plants. If you want to run the vines up tepee-shaped supports, dig holes in the corners of a 3-foot square and plant three pole bean seeds in each. Cover seeds 1 inch deep in clay soils, 1½ inches in sandy soils.

Care. To avoid the spread of diseases from plant to plant, cultivate shallowly and only when the foliage is dry. Water frequently by soaking the soil instead of sprinkling— moist foliage invites bacterial diseases (in humid areas) and mildew.

High-nitrogen fertilizers and heavy applications of compost will encourage more foliage growth than vegetable production. Use a fertilizer with a nitrogen-phosphorus-potassium ratio of 1:2:2, applying it every three to four weeks in a shallow furrow about 6 inches away from the plants. Cover the fertilizer band with soil. If you furrow-irrigate, apply the fertilizer in the furrows so water can carry it into the root zone of the bean plants.

Pests. Birds will often pull seedlings out of the ground. Cover the rows with an arched arbor of chicken wire to protect the seedlings until they are 6 inches high.

Several little round beetles and their larvae as well as several kinds of moth larvae feed on bean foliage and pods. Pick beetles off plants (some are nocturnal — find them by flashlight). If that isn't successful, control them with rotenone or malathion. (Follow label precautions so you spray far enough away from the harvest date.)

Nematodes can also be a problem on beans. They are tiny, round worms that make swellings on the roots of plants. Try to keep them out of your garden by making sure that plants and soil brought into your garden are uninfested. If nematodes do appear, marigolds planted in the infested area have been found to deter them. Persistent infestations can be cured by treating the soil with fumigants *before* planting.

Harvesting. Pick bean pods when they are at least 3 inches long but before they begin to get tough and stringy. At the ideal point, beans should be just starting to bulge the sides of the pods. The more faithful you are about frequent picking, the longer the plants will yield. Pull the pods off carefully while holding the fruiting stems with your free hand. This prevents breaking off stems and destroying plants.

In containers. Grow the bush forms of snap or lima beans, soybeans, or Southern peas in at least 8 to 12 inches of soil. For best results, add some garden soil to a commercial or homemade potting mix. The mix for soybeans should be especially fast draining.

SNAP BEANS

Often called string beans, these grow as self-supporting bushes or as climbing vines. The compact plant size, high productivity, and easy culture of bush beans make them one of the most popular of the summer vegetables. Runner or pole varieties require more work and attention because of the support needed by their long, twining vines, but they outyield bush varieties by a wide margin. Some pole varieties tend to be more flavorful than bush types. Although certain bush and runner varieties mentioned below are grown for shelled beans, their young pods are also delicious.

Since bush beans require only six to seven weeks to mature in warm weather, they can be grown successfully in areas with fairly short summers. Pole beans need from 10 days to 2 weeks more than bush types to fruit.

Recommended varieties. You can choose from a large list of bush beans: 'Bush Blue Lake', 'Cherokee Wax', 'Contender' (grows well under adverse conditions), 'Goldcrop' (yellow wax beans), 'Greencrop' (good flavor retention), 'Honey Gold', 'Kinghorn Wax' (plants reach 18 inches), 'Pencil Pod Wax' (yellow wax beans), 'Roma' (broad flat green pods with a distinctive flavor), 'Royalty' (dark purple pods; when cooked, the pods turn dark green), 'Tenderbest', 'Tendercrop' (disease resistant), 'Tenderette' (good flavor retention), 'Topcrop' (disease resistant).

Pole varieties include 'Blue Lake', 'Burpee Golden' (flat yellow pods), 'Kentucky Wonder', 'Oregon Giant' (shell beans), and 'Romano' or 'Italian' (broad, flat pods with a distinctive flavor).

LIMA BEANS

Both the bush and pole type of lima beans have larger and more spreading vines than their snap bean counterparts. Because they also mature three to five weeks later and require warmer soil to sprout reliably, lima beans are most successfully grown in areas where summers are long and rather warm.

Limas are planted much like snap beans except they need more space—plant them 4 to 6 inches apart in a row. In clay soils, plant seeds on edge to improve the chances of germination. Limas prefer a lean soil and should be

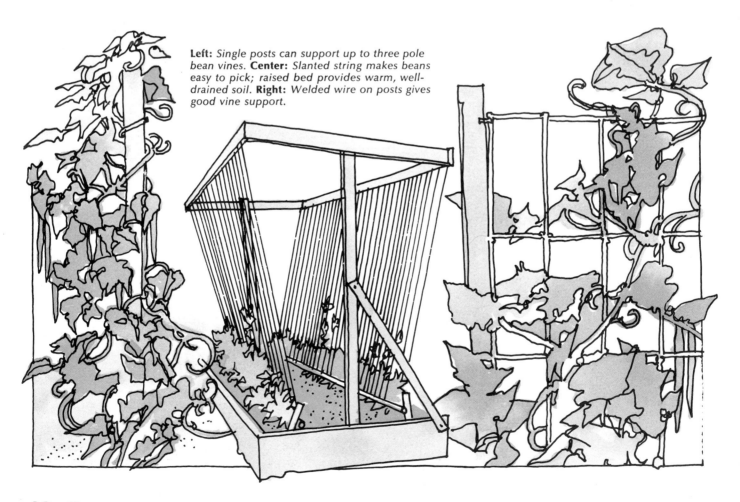

Left: *Single posts can support up to three pole bean vines.* **Center:** *Slanted string makes beans easy to pick; raised bed provides warm, well-drained soil.* **Right:** *Welded wire on posts gives good vine support.*

fertilized sparingly. Too much nitrogen results in heavy vine growth and few pods.

Pick the pods as soon as they begin to look a little lumpy from the swelling of seeds and before they begin to turn yellow. Keeping pods picked will prolong production. You can store sun-dried seeds for several months in sealed jars. Limas also lend themselves to canning or freezing.

Small-seeded baby limas or "butterbeans" are traditionally preferred in the Southeast. Plump-seeded "potato" limas are usually grown in other parts of the country.

Recommended varieties. Butterbeans: 'Florida Butter' (pole; speckled), 'Henderson Bush', 'Jackson Wonder' (bush; speckled), 'Small White' or 'Sieva' (pole). Potato limas: 'Dixie Butterpea' (bush), 'Fordhook 242' (bush; good heat resistance and heavy yields), 'King of the Garden' (pole), 'Large Speckled Christmas' (pole).

ASPARAGUS OR YARDLONG BEANS

This species is used in Oriental cooking. The plants, with their long runners and bean pods that reach 18 to 24 inches in length, somewhat resemble Southern peas. A long, warm season is required to mature this bean.

DRY BEANS

Culture is the same as for the bush type of snap beans. Let the beans remain on the bush until the pods turn dry or begin to shatter. Thresh them from their hulls and thoroughly dry them before storing for later use. Varieties include 'Dwarf Horticultural' (shell beans, bush), 'Great Northern', 'Pinto', 'Red Kidney', and 'White Marrowfat'.

SOYBEANS

The green seeds are shelled from the short, plump, furry pods and cooked for their high protein and oil content. Soybeans grow best in the warm, humid South and Midwest and do poorly in most dry climates. Grow them much as you would bush lima beans; the bushes are about the same size.

BROAD BEANS OR FAVA BEANS

The name comes from the long, rather broad, flattened green pods that are shelled to produce large, meaty seeds. They require long periods of cool weather to mature. Plant them in late summer or fall in mild-winter climates and in very early spring elsewhere. The plants grow 3 to 4½ feet high.

SOUTHERN PEAS OR COWPEAS

Although referred to as "peas" in the Southern states, these plants more closely approximate beans in appearance and cultural requirements. Tropical in origin, Southern peas need about four months of warm days and nights to set good crops of pods.

Generally available varieties, such as 'Blackeye', 'Chowder', and 'Purple Hull', have large, spreading plants, 2 feet or more in height. Newer varieties mature earlier and have more compact plants.

Harvest and shell peas before the pods turn yellow, or let overly mature pods dry and shell for winter storage.

FLAGEOLETS

Popular in France, flageolets have a creamy texture and mellow flavor when they're shelled, simmered in water for about 1½ hours, and served with butter. Plant seeds in spring (after the soil has warmed up) in rich soil an inch deep and 3 inches apart in rows 2½ feet apart. Make furrows before planting for deep watering.

Beets

Plant seeds from spring through fall as long as the weather is cool. Use roots and tops in 6 to 8 weeks.

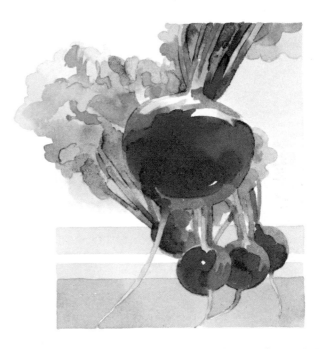

Beets are a little slow to sprout from their corky seeds but, once started, grow rapidly and produce a great deal of delicious food in a small amount of space. They attract few pests and tolerate warm, but prefer cool, weather. (Where summers are very hot, plant beets to mature before and after hot weather.) You can eat both the roots and the immature tops.

You can grow winter crops of beets in mild climates; seeds should be sown in early fall and the roots harvested before they begin to shoot up seed stalks the following spring.

Recommended varieties. 'Burpee Golden' (golden yellow roots), 'Detroit Dark Red', 'Early Wonder', 'Firechief', 'Formanova' (large cylindrical roots allow uniform slices),

'Green Top Bunching' (beautiful green leaves), 'Lutz Green Leaf' (beautiful green foliage; beets good for winter storage), 'Ruby Queen'.

How to plant. To maintain a supply of beets throughout the summer, plant seeds in short rows as early as the soil can be worked in the spring and at monthly intervals until late summer. In hot summer areas, plant beets in early spring prior to 80° F. weather. Cover seeds with ¼ inch of sand, vermiculite, or finely pulverized compost to improve germination. Sow seeds 1 inch apart. Thin to at least 2 inches apart when plants are small, using the greens. Space rows 1½ to 2 feet apart.

Care. Beets need frequent watering in dry weather to keep the roots tender and plump.

Light applications of a complete fertilizer every 3 to 4 weeks help the roots form quickly and remain tender.

Pests. Beets interest few pests except a kind of grub called a root maggot and slugs that can burrow into roots or spoil the tops of small plants. Root maggots can be discouraged by digging in heavy applications of compost and by not planting root crops in the same location each year. Look for slugs and hand pick them.

Harvesting. Begin pulling beets to eat as soon as they reach 1 inch in diameter; this will make room for the remaining roots to grow to their mature size of 2 to 3 inches in diameter. When beets are tiny, both tops and roots can be cooked together. Don't let beets grow to jumbo sizes; they can develop streaks of woody tissue.

In containers. Beets will thrive in planter boxes deep enough for their roots (about 12 inches). Give them 3 inches between plants.

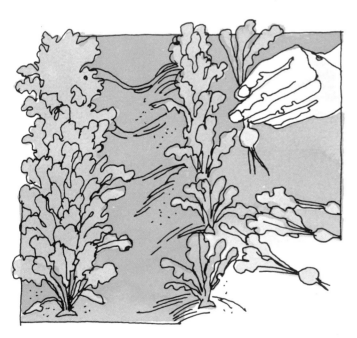

Thin beets *when they are 1 inch in diameter; this allows remaining roots to reach mature size. You can eat thinnings.*

Broccoli

Hardy cabbage relative. Start plants to mature during cool weather but before severe frosts.

This cool-season crop bears over a long period of time. The leafy, erect plants reach from 1½ to 2 feet tall. Broccoli has been much improved in recent years through the efforts of plant breeders developing better varieties for commercial freezing. They increased the size and holding ability of the central head and reduced plant size. Once the central head is removed side shoots can produce additional heads.

Frost-hardy broccoli plants should be transplanted to the garden in early spring to mature ahead of hot days or in early fall so they will be ready for harvest before killing frost. In mild Western climates, winter broccoli can be grown successfully, but plants should begin to head before the onset of cold weather. The optimum temperature range for growing broccoli is 40° to 70° F.

Recommended varieties. 'Calabrese' (produces many side shoots), 'Cleopatra' (tolerant of cold temperatures and drought; produces good side shoots), 'De Cicco' (produces many side shoots), 'De Rapa' (one of the original Italian sprouting types that does not form large central heads), 'Green Comet' (heat and disease resistant), 'Green Mountain', 'Neptune', 'Premium Crop' (heads resist premature bud opening), 'Waltham 29'.

How to plant. Grow spring broccoli from started plants; start fall or winter broccoli from seeds sown in the garden in late summer. Where summers aren't too warm, sow seed in the garden in early spring. Sow seeds ½ inch deep and 1 inch apart. Later transplant or thin plants to 16 inches apart; spacing between rows should be 2½ to 3 feet. Spring broccoli will mature in 50 to 60 days; winter crops need 75 to 90 days to form heads.

Care. Give broccoli plenty of water and push it along with frequent applications of high-nitrogen plant food to develop the big, vigorous plants that are necessary to support large heads. Plant short rows; six plants are sufficient to feed four people. To avoid having many heads maturing at once, you can plant three broccoli plants at 3-week intervals.

Pests. Broccoli heads are so large and tight that cabbage worms and aphids can be difficult to eliminate. Try hosing off aphids or using a soapy solution on them (see page 22). If you use malathion, spray before heads form and follow label precautions. Control cabbage worms with a spray of the biological insecticide *Bacillus thuringiensis*.

Harvesting. Cut the central heads while the buds are still tight. Include up to 6 inches of the edible stem and leaves. Pierce the lower stem with your thumbnail; peel off and discard the skin where it is hard and woody. Broccoli will send up edible shoots after you harvest the central head. Keeping shoots harvested before flowering will encourage production as long as the weather is cool. When the weather warms, the heat will force broccoli to flower — then it's past the good-eating stage.

In containers. Large plants make broccoli impractical for containers.

To harvest broccoli, *cut off central stalk before buds begin to open; use a sharp knife. Harvesting encourages side shoots.*

Brussels sprouts

A plant set out in spring or fall can provide a hundred tiny sprouts as long as the weather stays cool.

This member of the cabbage family produces edible "sprouts" that look like tiny cabbages. Not everyone can grow sprouts because of their preference for a long growing period of cool weather. The plants grow large and the sprouts cluster tightly around the tall main stem, maturing from the base up. Harvesting can continue for many weeks. Four to six plants can feed four people.

Recommended varieties. 'Jade Cross Hybrid' (a heavy producer; can be started early enough for short-season areas), 'Long Island Improved'.

How to plant. Where summers are short but cool, purchase plants early and transplant them to the garden as soon as the soil can be worked in the spring. Protect plants on very cold nights by placing wide-mouth glass jars over them. Remove these during the day so the plants don't cook. (Light frosts won't harm the plants.)

Four to five months of cool weather are required for Brussels sprouts to mature from seeds. In California's coastal belt, start seeds in the garden in late summer; elsewhere set out plants so the sprouts will mature during cool weather. Plant seeds ½ inch deep. Transplant to stand 2 to 2½ feet apart; leave 3 feet between rows.

Care. Give sprouts ample water and encourage growth with frequent applications of a high-nitrogen fertilizer. Remove leaves from all but the top of the plant as sprouts crowd them.

Pests. Try to keep aphids hosed off before they get inside the sprouts.

Harvesting. Snap or trim off the sprouts when they are firm and still deep green; they are at their best when about 1 to 1½ inches in diameter. A well-grown plant can yield 75 to 100 sprouts over a 30 to 45-day period. Mild frosts improve their flavor, but where winters are severe, the harvest can be prolonged by uprooting the plants with a spade, snapping off the leaves, laying the plants on a bed of straw or leaves, covering the roots with soil, and spreading 6 to 12 inches of straw or leaves over the plants to insulate them.

In containers. Large plant requires a massive container, but high yield makes growing one plant worthwhile.

Cabbage

Space-eater; pests love it; but delicious, abundant crops reward you in cool weather.

Top left: *savoy* **Top right:** *red*
Center: *green*
Bottom: *Chinese*

If you have judged cabbage by the pale, often strong-tasting heads sold commercially, you will be surprised to discover the delicious flavor of the vegetable when home grown, as well as the variety of rich colors and leaf textures available. You can choose from among several red

varieties and the crinkly leafed Savoy varieties, in addition to the green cabbages.

Cabbage should be planted to mature during cool weather. You can grow spring and fall crops where the cool but frost-free growing season is 5 months or more in length. Plant early varieties or hybrids in the spring; these mature in 7 to 8 weeks from transplants. Later varieties, such as the king-size kraut cabbage, need up to 12 weeks to mature from seeds and should be planted after midsummer for fall harvest. Winter cabbage can be grown in mild-climate areas, but the heads tend to burst and send up flower stalks as a result of warm spells.

Recommended varieties. Early miniatures: 'Dwarf Morden', 'Earliana'. Early to midseason varieties: 'Early Jersey Wakefield' (resistant to yellows disease), 'Emerald Cross', 'Golden Acre' (resistant to yellows disease), 'Greenback', 'Harvester Queen' (heat and disease resistant), 'King Cole', 'Salad Green' (for cole slaw), 'Stonehead' (firm heads that develop well in heat). Red types: 'Red Head' (good winter variety), 'Ruby Head' (heat resistant). Late-maturing varieties: 'Premium Flat Dutch', 'Savoy Chieftain'. Savoy types: 'Savoy Ace' (develops early), 'Savoy King'.

How to plant. Plant cabbage in a different spot every year to avoid pests. Spring cabbage is usually grown from plants to gain three to four weeks time. Grow fall cabbage from seeds sown in the garden after midsummer. When buying spring cabbage plants, look for a light purple cast to the leaves. This indicates that they have been properly hardened off.

Plant seeds ½ inch deep. Transplant them 24 to 30 inches apart, with 36 inches between rows. Early cabbage can be spaced 18 inches apart. Make sure to set in the plants to the same depth that they grew in the flat and to firm the soil around the roots.

Care. Grow cabbage rapidly with frequent light applications of high-nitrogen fertilizer and regular watering. Cabbage responds favorably to the cool, moist soil conditions produced by a mulch of hay or straw.

Pests. Aphids are prevalent and persistent pests. Control them with a soapy water spray (see page 22) or use rotenone or malathion (note label precautions).

The most serious pest of the cabbage is the green cabbage worm, the larva of a small, white butterfly often found hovering over cabbage patches in late spring. Cabbage worm feeds on the tender young leaves, producing ragged holes, and often burrows into the heads. Good control can be achieved by using one of the dusts or sprays for chewing insects; *Bacillus thuringiensis* and rotenone are effective.

You can control cabbage root maggot, a small, yellowish white maggot that tunnels into the roots and causes plants to wilt, by spraying the ground around young seedlings with diazinon.

Harvesting. Begin harvesting heads when they are firm and about the size of a softball. Cut just beneath the head, leaving some basal leaves to support new growth of small lateral heads. (See Brussels sprouts for directions for storing heads.) A light frost won't hurt them, but don't allow the heads to freeze before harvest.

In containers: Deep roots and large heads make most cabbage impractical for containers. Exceptions are flowering and miniature forms or Chinese cabbage harvested while young for salad greens.

CHINESE CABBAGE

The main secret to successful culture of this delicious vegetable is the planting date. Except for some hybrids, Chinese cabbage quickly shoots up flower heads during the long days of summer, so spring plantings are risky except in the cool northern tier of states or along the Western coast fog belt. Elsewhere, delay planting until after midsummer, when the shortening days and cool weather will permit heads to grow to a large size before extremely cold weather freezes them. Chinese cabbage matures in 65 to 80 days from seeds sown in the garden.

Plant seeds ½ inch deep in garden rows about 2 feet apart. Eat the excess seedlings and let the remainder stand 12 to 18 inches apart. Fertilize and water frequently to sustain rapid growth. Pests are few except for the worm-like cabbage loopers; spray with *Bacillus thuringiensis* (note label precautions).

Recommended varieties. 'Michihli' has long, slender, tapering heads. 'Wong Bok' is short and barrel shaped, very desirable because of high proportion of green leaf area to white stem.

Carrots

Two secrets to success with carrots: keep seeds moist until they're up; provide loose soil for long roots.

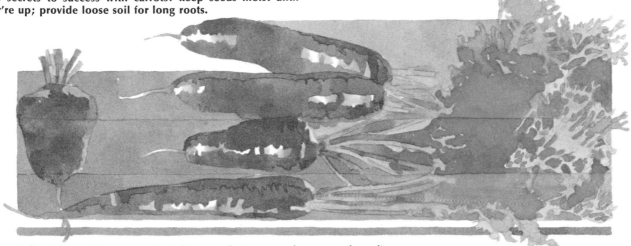

Left: *Oxheart (short rooted).* **Right top to bottom:** *medium rooted, medium rooted, short rooted, long rooted*

Few other vegetables can match home grown carrots for vitamin content and sweet flavor. Carrots have the happy habit of remaining in good condition long after maturity, so roots are rarely wasted. And even though carrots prefer cool weather, crops can be grown in midsummer in all areas of the country but the South. In mild-winter areas, if you plant carrots in early fall, the roots will continue to grow slowly during the winter, insuring a steady supply for salads, stews, and carrot sticks. Most varieties require 65 to 75 days to grow to full size.

Recommended varieties. Long rooted (up to 9 inches): 'Gold Pak', 'Imperator'. Medium rooted (6 to 7 inches): 'Goldinhart', 'Nantes' (both are very sweet and tender). Short rooted (4 to 5 inches): 'Burpee's Oxheart', 'Little Finger', 'Red-cored Chantenay', 'Short 'N' Sweet', 'Tiny Sweet'. (These varieties work well in heavy clay or shallow rocky soils.)

How to plant. From the size of the mature carrot root, you could guess that they would need deep, porous soil to develop to full size. Adding a thin layer of topsoil won't do; you have to open up the hard clay or silt soils to a 1-foot depth by spading in organic matter, such as well-rotted manure or peat moss. Too much coarse compost, however, will cause carrot roots to fork. Minimize soil compaction by laying boards between the rows to walk on. Or try the sand trench method by planting seeds ½ inch deep in a trench of sand 2 inches wide and 8 inches deep. Feeder roots will grow sideways through the sand and draw nutrients from the soil.

Plant seeds ½ inch deep and ½ inch apart; later thin to 2 inches and finally to 3 inches as you remove half-grown roots for kitchen use. Space rows about 12 inches apart. Germination can fail in dry weather when the soil dries out quickly and crusts form. You can improve sprouting by covering the seeded furrow with a board or plastic sheet as explained on page 15. Seedlings look almost grasslike when the first leaves emerge, so weed carefully.

Starting carrot seeds in pots and transplanting them to the garden has some advantages over sowing seeds directly in the ground. Because germination is more certain in pots, you save on seeds. You also save the labor of early weeding and thinning. Still another advantage: you can sow at any time of the year.

Sow 10 to 12 seeds evenly in a 4 to 6-inch pot. Keep the soil damp, thinning to six or eight evenly spaced carrots per pot. Set out by planting the entire clump in the planting hole, turning it out of the pot carefully to avoid breaking the soil ball. Harvest the whole clump at once.

If you want a continuous supply of carrots, you can plant seeds at three week intervals; avoid hot summer months and winter months with freezing temperatures.

Care. Carrots respond to frequent light applications of fertilizer and regular watering by developing large and tender roots. Rough roots can result from prolonged wet, cool weather. Twisted, distorted roots are often caused by delaying thinning too long. Forking and branching roots result from the use of fresh manure, rough, slow-decaying compost, or layers of hard soil. And infrequent watering can cause cracking of roots; the hard roots can literally swell and burst open when they finally get water.

Pests. Carrot rust fly is the one enemy which can be considered serious. Its larvae tunnel into roots of carrots. This is primarily a warm-weather pest; plant carrots to mature in cool weather so grubs won't disfigure them. Or try digging in lots of well-rotted compost to encourage natural predators.

Harvesting. Begin pulling carrots as soon as roots reach finger size, harvesting all roots before seed heads form. If the soil is a little hard, prying roots with a trowel as you pull up on the tops will prevent them from breaking off; or water before pulling. If you do break off a top, dig out and eat the root; it may not grow a new top.

Carrot roots are easy to store where winters are severe (elsewhere, leave them in the ground). Before the soil freezes, dig the roots, break off the heavy part of the tops, and store the roots in dry sand or in leaf or straw pits or piles, as described on page 24.

In containers. Short varieties and miniatures are best. Soil should be at least 12 inches deep and very loose.

Cauliflower

Late summer is a good time to set out plants in most areas. Harvest in 2 to 3 months.

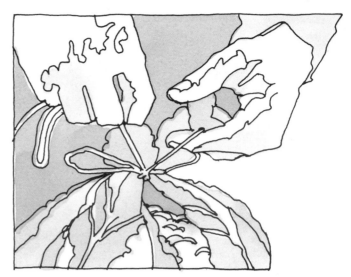

To blanch cauliflower, *gather large outer leaves over head and secure them with heavy twine, string, or a wide rubber band.*

A cool-weather crop grown for early summer and fall harvest, cauliflower will flower rapidly if the weather turns hot. Winter harvests are possible in mild Western or Gulf Coast climates. Plants are fairly frost hardy. Allow 60 to 80 days from transplanting to harvest—90 to 100 days for winter crops. See broccoli for culture, care, and pest control.

Start cauliflower from small plants set out 18 to 20 inches apart in rows 2 to 2½ feet apart. Keep plants actively growing; any growth check might cause premature setting of undersized heads.

Unlike broccoli, with its erect plants, cauliflower forms its edible buds only a few inches above the ground. Blanching of heads whitens them by excluding light and can be done simply by gathering the long wrapper leaves and securing them at the top with a wide rubber band. This prevents the formation of green or purplish pigment. Unwrap the heads occasionally to check for pests. Begin the blanching process when the bud clusters are about 2 inches in diameter. Blanching takes from 1 to 2 weeks time. If you tie up several heads, it's helpful to label each one so you'll know when to harvest them.

If the weather does turn hot, an overhead sprinkling will create the humidity that cauliflower needs. But don't substitute this for deep soaking.

Harvest heads before the bud segments or ''curds'' begin to separate in preparation for shooting up flower heads.

Recommended varieties. 'Purple Head' (large plants with heads in a deep purple color that turn green when cooked and have a flavor somewhat like broccoli; needs no blanching), 'Self Blanching' (leaves grow upward, curving over the heads and naturally blanching the heads), 'Snowball', 'Snow Crown' (an early variety that performs well under adverse conditions), 'Snow King' (heat tolerant and disease resistant).

In containers. Large size of each plant makes cauliflower impractical in containers.

Celery

Well-developed stalks demand rich soil, ample water and nutrients, and a long, cool season. Slow-growing crop; buying plants speeds results.

If your area enjoys about four months of cool weather and if you can provide a deep bed of sandy or organic soil, you can grow celery rather easily. Elsewhere you may end up with tough stalks on plants that go to seed. Instead of being a total loss, however, leaves, stalks, and seeds all make good flavoring.

Celeriac — a close relative — is grown like celery. It forms rough, knobby, rounded roots that are peeled and used in soups and stews. Since plants are seldom available, grow celeriac from seeds.

Recommended varieties. 'Burpee's Golden Self-Blanching' (stalks naturally blanch to a clear yellow), 'Giant Pascal' (seeds and plants generally available), 'Golden Detroit' (stalks are pale gold; a self-blanching variety), 'Slow Bolt' (used where early spring-planted celery is subject to light frosts), 'Summer Pascal' (green-stalked variety; often used without blanching), 'Tall Utah' (seeds and plants generally available).

How to plant. In hot climates, best results come from seeds or transplants started in late summer. In mild West Coast areas you can grow celery almost year round. If you're in doubt about your winter's effect, try glass or plastic frost protectors (see pages 15, 17); or start seeds indoors in January and set out seedlings in early spring.

If you use seeds, soak them first. They germinate in about 10 days, are ready to transplant into the ground when they are about 3 inches high, in 10 to 12 weeks. Sometimes nurseries sell seedlings in 2-inch pots or six-packs.

Work in plenty of fertilizer and soil conditioners before transplanting celery into the ground. Space plants about 6 inches apart, rows about 2½ to 3 feet apart. Stagger the harvest period by transplanting only a half dozen or so at one time. Make furrows between rows and irrigate thoroughly and often. (If plants dry out, they get tough.)

Care. When plants are about half mature size (about 2½ months after transplanting), begin forcing them to grow rapidly. Feed and water frequently.

Blanching celery produces white stalks. When the weather begins to cool in fall, shade the base of the stalks with boards or mounds of soil or straw.

Pests. Celery worm, the colorful larva of the black swallowtail butterfly, may feed on celery foliage. If they do serious damage, remove them by hand or spray with *Bacillus thuringiensis*.

Harvesting. Some gardeners harvest a few stalks at a time as soon as they look ready; others wait until the plant forms a tight head, then cut off the whole thing just above the roots. New stalks grow from the roots; they are smaller and less succulent than the first stalks.

Surplus fall-crop heads can be stored for weeks if dug up, roots and all, before frost and kept in a well-ventilated, cool place. Or heads can be protected in place by piling straw against them and holding it down with soil.

In containers. Although celery can succeed in deep containers, plants need even more watering and feeding than they do in the ground. This results in a great deal of maintenance over a long growing period.

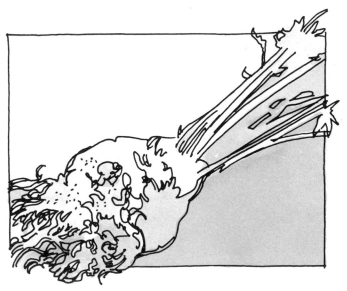

Celeriac, *a celery relative, forms rough, knobby, rounded roots that are peeled for use. Grow celeriac from seed.*

Chard

All the same uses as spinach but not as fussy about weather or soil. Plant seeds in spring and summer.

Top: *white ribbed.* **Bottom:** *rhubarb*

Few vegetables can match Swiss chard for ease of growth and heavy, extended production of delicious, crinkly green leaves and wide, crisp stems. Six to eight plants can feed a family for several months because new center leaves continually replace the large outer leaves as they are harvested.

A member of the beet family, chard can be harvested 60 days following spring planting or 45 days after summer planting. Plants withstand summer heat in most areas, yet will mature by midsummer where summers are cool.

Recommended varieties. 'Fordhook Giant', 'Lucullus', 'Rhubarb' (has red stems and ribs and dark green leaves; plant is decorative enough to be used in groups among flowers), 'White Ribbed'.

How to plant. Grow chard from seeds sown outdoors as soon as the soil can be worked in the spring. In mild-winter areas, chard can be planted any time of the year, but fall plantings shoot to seed the following spring. Plant seeds ½ inch deep and 1 inch apart. Thin plants to 8 to 12 inches apart; eat the excess plants. Rows should be spaced about 20 inches apart. Chard seeds are well adapted to band planting or broadcasting.

Care. Feed chard every two to three weeks with a complete fertilizer, and water frequently. The plants may wilt slightly on hot days but will recover quickly if the soil around them is soaked.

Pests. Chard is virtually pest-free. If aphids attack the plants, blast them off with a fine, sharp spray of water.

Harvesting. Harvest the outer leaves as needed and before the stems get stringy. Break or cut them off at the base. Replacement leaves will grow from the center. Always leave a few center leaves so the plants can manufacture sugars to sustain themselves.

In containers. No other vegetable can match chard for sustained heavy yield from a small space. Use containers with a soil depth of 12 to 24 inches. If you remove the outer leaves to use, the plant will continue to grow.

Collards

Plant seeds of this "headless cabbage" for cool-weather maturity. Flavor is improved by light frosts.

Grown all over the country for its succulent greens or leaves, this cabbage relative is most popular in the South, where it's summer planted for fall and winter harvest. The mature plants are frost hardy and yield sweet leaves after cold weather has concentrated their sugars.

Collards look like lanky, open-growing, nonheading cabbages. The plants can reach 2 to 3 feet in height. Although collards bear a superficial resemblance to their close relative, kale, their flavor is distinctly unique.

Recommended varieties. 'Georgia' (non-heading variety that tolerates heat and poor soils; is taller than 'Vates'), 'Vates' (compact variety with large, slightly crumpled leaves).

How to plant. In areas with short, cool summers, plant seeds outdoors in late spring. Elsewhere, plant after midsummer. Sow seeds ½ inch deep and 1 inch apart. Thin to 18 to 24 inches apart; eat thinnings for greens.

Care. Keep the stems and leaves tender by watering and feeding frequently. The large leaves evaporate a lot of water, so soak the soil deeply. Feed every three to four weeks with a high-nitrogen fertilizer.

Pests. Collards have the same pests as cabbage; use the same controls.

Harvesting. Don't harvest the first six to eight leaves on the plants; let them develop to full size to sustain the plants. Clip off and cook younger leaves, including the stems, when they are about the size of your hand. If you harvest larger, older leaves, discard the stringy stems and test the leaf midrib for tenderness to see if it should be saved. Never harvest the central growing point or you will delay the production of new leaves until side shoots are formed.

In containers. Plants are large but will yield a continuous supply of greens in large tubs or deep boxes.

Corn

You need warm weather and a soil area big enough for at least three rows.

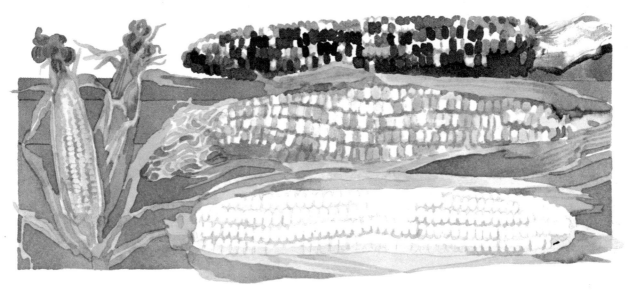

Left: *yellow.* **Right top to bottom:** *Indian, honey and cream, white*

If garden-fresh sweet corn tastes better to you than the "store-bought" kind, you're not just imagining it. Unless corn ears are cooled to remove field heat immediately after harvesting, they begin at once to lose sugar.

Corn is a heat-loving vegetable. Untreated seeds won't sprout reliably until the soil reaches 60° to 65°. Extra-early hybrids (small plants with rather small ears) mature in about 60 days. The second-early or midseason maincrop hybrids mature in 65 to 80 days and have medium-size to rather large ears and plants that reach 6 feet or more in height. Late varieties and hybrids require 90 days or more to harvest; most are tall plants.

Recommended varieties. Open-pollinated and non-hybrid varieties mature later, bear smaller ears, and show less disease resistance than most hybrids. Hybrids are selected not only for high row count and long ears but also for depth of kernels. Generally, the later the hybrid matures, the larger and longer the ears and deeper the kernels.

Hybrids are available with golden, white, and bicolored ears. Each type has a distinct flavor. All are good but the "super sweet" hybrids are superior. Unless your growing season is very short, don't rely on the extra-early hybrids for your main crop, because they are low yielding. Don't plant late varieties if you live in an area where summers are short. Don't plant the super-sweet or extra-sweet hybrids near any other corn, or crossing will spoil the flavor. Popcorn, too, needs a separation of at least 300 feet from sweet corn.

Early: 'Early Sunglow' (grows well in cool weather; plants reach 4½ feet in height), 'Early Xtra Sweet' (very sweet kernels; retains sweetness for a long time), 'Golden Beauty' (plants grow to 5½ feet), 'Golden Midget' (tiny ears to 4½ inches; plants grow to 3 feet), 'Morning Sun', 'Polar Vee', 'Seneca 60'. Midseason: 'Butter & Sugar' (bicolor), 'F M Cross', 'Golden Cross Bantam', 'Golden Jubilee', 'Honey and Cream' (yellow and white kernels), 'Super Sweet'. Late: 'Country Gentleman' (white kernels; good for canning and freezing), 'Illini Xtra Sweet' (high sugar content; sweetness is retained longer than most sweet varieties), 'Iochief' (large ears; wind-resistant stalks), 'Silver Queen' (white kernels), 'Stylepak' (8-inch ears that are good for canning and freezing; husks keep tips from drying out).

How to plant. Corn should be planted in a block of at least three rows (rather than in one row) to insure pollination. Corn pollen from the tassels must fall on the silks of the ears before kernels (seeds) will form. Wet or very

Left: *Furrow watering gives corn — a large thirsty vegetable — deep soaking it needs. Dig furrows at planting time.*
Top right: *Dry brown silks indicate ripe corn.* **Bottom right:** *Corn at most tender stage spurts milky juice when pierced.*

hot weather can interfere with pollination. Missing kernels or poorly filled out ears can result from poor pollination or nutrient deficiencies. Providing you have the room, you can keep a constant supply of corn coming from midsummer until fall either by planting small blocks of one to two dozen plants every two weeks or by mixing seeds of hybrids of various maturity dates. Follow the latter course only if you plant a large block of at least three or four dozen plants to minimize pollination problems.

In climates where rain comes in the summer, gardeners generally plant rows or hills (see page 15) on flat ground and supply water with sprinklers if and when it's needed. But in dry-summer climates, it's best to prepare for a summer of heavy watering by building irrigation furrows at planting time (see page 15).

Use strings to line up straight rows in moist spaded or tilled ground, scoop out a trench, and pile soil along the rim of the trench. Space rows 30 to 36 inches apart. Plant seeds 4 to 6 inches apart.

Use your fingers or a trowel to bury seeds 1 to 2 inches deep in the shoulder of the excavated soil. Make sure you place the seed well down into moist soil. The seeds should sprout in four to seven days.

Unless it's very hot, seedlings usually won't need water until they grow 3 or 4 inches tall. As soon as soil around the seeds begins to dry out to a depth of 2 or 3 inches, fill furrows with water. Don't let seedlings wilt.

In dry-summer climates, water is the most important part of growing. After seedlings are up and growing vigorously, it's difficult to give them too much water, and dangerous to give them too little. In places where summers are rainy or cool, you may not have to water at all or only once or twice during the season.

Don't worry if corn leaves wilt in the hot part of the day; the root system isn't efficient enough to send water (even if plenty is there) up to the top of the plant. However, you should water right away if the plant has not recovered its freshness the next morning.

Care. When seedlings reach about 6 inches tall, give them more room by thinning them to stand 8 to 12 inches apart (closer for the more compact varieties).

Corn needs a good amount of fertilizer. Mixing in compost, manure, or fertilizer before planting may be enough, but in addition to, or in place of that, you generally should feed once during the season. Scatter complete fertilizer in furrows and water it in or apply liquid food in the furrows. Feed anytime between when the plants are 12 inches tall and when tassels form.

Weeds compete with young corn but usually get shaded out as the stalks grow. Shallowly hoe weeds every week for the first six or eight weeks. At the same time scrape loose soil onto the hills around the plants.

Pests. Corn earworm is the worst corn pest. The adult moth lays eggs on the silks and the eggs hatch into worms that crawl into the ear to eat the kernels.

One way to reduce worm damage is to cut off the silks about three days after the ears reach full size. If you cut the silks off too soon, you'll get ears with kernels missing.

Another way to reduce earworm damage: using a medicine dropper, put ¼ teaspoon of mineral oil on the silks of each ear after pollination. The oil smothers earworm eggs.

Harvesting. Timing is critical because the sugar in the kernels turns to starch as soon as the ear is picked or reaches a certain age. In warm weather, corn will be ready to eat about three weeks after you see the yellow pollen flying. When the silks dry up, slit the shucks and inspect the kernels for harvest readiness. They should be large and well colored but not tough when tested with your thumbnail. Milky juice spurts out if the ear is at the best eating stage. Clear juice means wait a few days. If the juice looks like toothpaste, you're too late.

Pop the harvested ears into ice water if you can't cook, freeze, or can them immediately. This will slow the conversion from sugar to starch. If you slip and let kernels get past the juicy "milk" and into the drier "dough" stage, you can still add milk and use the kernels for creamed corn.

In containers. Midget varieties, such as 'Golden Midget', yield best results in containers. Several tubs with at least three plants each will insure good pollination. Stalks require regular feeding and watering to set ears.

Cress

Flavor resembles watercress. Easy to grow as long as the weather is cool. Sow seeds in early spring.

In this salad-minded era, cress should not be overlooked as a nippy garnish. Upland or curly cress (small, parsley-like plants) grows easily and rapidly from seeds sown outdoors in cool weather. Plant seeds in rows about 18 inches apart; thin plants to 6 to 8 inches apart.

In containers. Try growing cress indoors in a shallow tray. Sprinkle seeds on wet cheesecloth that has been spread on top of potting mix. Keep the cheesecloth moist and sticking to the soil surface. Snip seedlings to use in 10 to 14 days.

Cucumbers

As big as blackjacks or as small as your little finger; shaped like baby blimps, fat cigars, or even lemons; smooth or "warty"; for slicing or pickling—all grow fast in warm weather.

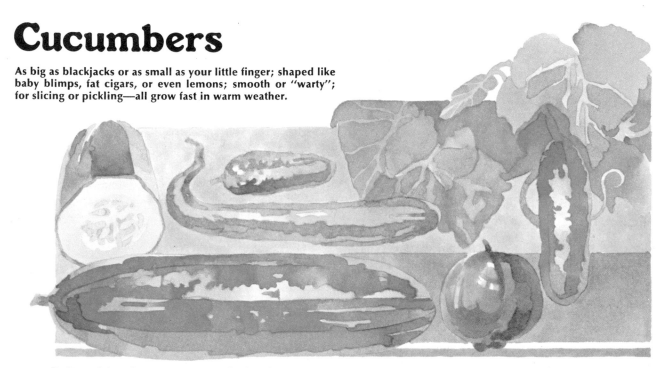

Left to right: *slicing, Armenian, gherkin, lemon, slicing*

If you like to fill shelves with jars of garden vegetables for winter use, plant cucumbers. Six to twelve vines will keep you busy pickling for several weeks. The vines of most varieties will spread over 6 feet before the plants are worn out from heavy bearing. Standard vining cucumbers are not for the small garden unless you can train them up supports.

Each cucumber vine bears both male and female flowers; female blossoms are recognizable by the swollen ovary just behind the flower. Pollen is transferred from male flowers by insects and wind. Certain hybrids have been selected for their high percentage of female flowers; seedsmen will usually mix in a few seeds of a male pollinator variety to insure fruiting. Fruits won't set without pollination; poorly formed fruits are usually caused by nutritional problems, too little or too much water, or hot weather.

Recommended varieties. Slicing varieties grow 6 to 9 inches in length. Young fruits can be pickled whole or the mature cucumbers sliced crosswise or into sticks for ease of packing into jars. 'Armenian' (oriental type with long, ribbed, light green fruit; reputedly easy to digest), 'Burpee Hybrid' (8-inch fruit; resistant to mosaic virus and downy mildew), 'Burpless Hybrid' (10-inch fruit; reputedly easy to digest), 'Bush Whopper' (plant forms a compact bush 3 feet in diameter; good in containers; resistant to scab and mosaic virus), 'Gemini Hybrid' (produces high percentage of female flowers; resistant to scab and mosaic virus, anthracnose, downy and powdery mildew), 'Lemon' (fruit resembles a large lemon, has a sweet flavor; harvest when fruit is yellow), 'Marketer' (white-spined, smooth, slender fruit; resistant to downy mildew and mosaic virus), 'Palomar' (disease resistant), 'Spartan Valor Hybrid' (produces high percentage of female flowers; long, dark green fruit; resistant to scab and mosaic virus), 'Victory' (produces high percentage of female flowers; disease resistant).

Pickling varieties have short, blocky fruits which are slightly more prolific than the slicers and are more convenient for making whole pickles. 'Bravo' (hybrid bred for the Southeast), 'Cherokee' (short, 3-foot vines; hybrid bred for the Southeast), 'Crispy' (disease resistant), 'Ohio MR 17' (very productive; fruit can be used for small or large pickles; resistant to mosaic virus), 'Peppi' (early compact hybrid variety; produces long fruit), 'Pioneer Hybrid' (good for Northern climates; fruit ripens for pickling within a 2-week period; resistant to scab and mosaic virus, downy and powdery mildew), 'Wisconsin SMR 18' (favorite for commercial picklers; resistant to scab and mosaic virus).

The new compact hybrids for small gardens, hanging baskets, and container growing include these three varieties: 'Little Minnie', 'Tiny Dill', and the early, disease-resistant 'Patio Pik'.

How to plant. Cucumbers are definitely a warm-weather vegetable. The seeds need warm soil to sprout (use hot-caps and other similar devices; see pages 14–15), and the plants need warm weather to help pollination. (Pollina-tion can be inhibited, though, by extreme dryness combined with heat.)

Plant the seeds 1 inch deep and 2 to 3 inches apart in a row and later thin to 12 inches apart. Space rows 4 to 5 feet apart. Closer spacing can increase yields, especially if you create a rich, fast-draining soil by incorporating lots of organic matter and if you mulch under the vines with straw.

If you expect some cool spells during the growing season, plant the seeds along fences where reflected heat will encourage faster growth and better fruiting. You can also start seeds indoors in peat pots 2 to 3 weeks before the usual date of the last spring frost (see pages 12–13 for further information).

Care. Cucumbers need lots of water. Sprinkling is not recommended for most gardens because it encourages mildew. Furrow irrigation works best but vines can clog the furrows. Train all the vines in one direction to keep the irrigation furrow open. In small gardens, train the vines up 3 to 5-foot-high vertical or slanted frames covered with chicken wire or strung with stout twine. Cucumber vines don't cling; tie them up every foot or so. Pinch out the tips of rambling vines; this will cause more branches to form. Feed every three to four weeks by scattering a complete fertilizer in the irrigation furrow and watering deeply.

Pests. Cucumber beetles feed on the leaves and can spread bacterial wilt, a fatal cucumber disease for which there is no known cure. The larva of the beetle also does damage, boring into the roots. Dust with diazinon or sevin (follow label precautions). Dusts are preferable to sprays, since moisture can cause mildew on cucumber plants. Cucumber beetle will usually show up only while plants are young.

Harvesting. With most varieties, pick for sweet pickles when 2 or 3 inches long, for dills when 5 or 6 inches, for slicing when 6 to 8 inches. Pick cucumbers before they begin to turn yellow, because at the yellow stage the seeds begin to harden. Keep fruits picked—leaving older fruits on vines inhibits the formation of new fruit. Hold the brittle vines firmly while twisting or clipping off the fruits to prevent breakage.

In containers. Try compact varieties, such as 'Bush Whopper', 'Little Minnie', 'Patio Pik', and 'Tiny Dill', in good-size tubs or barrels. Include plenty of well-rotted manure or compost in the potting mix and feed plants frequently.

ARMENIAN CUCUMBER

Plant seeds of this mild-tasting cucumber as you would those of any other cucumber. The vine will spread 4 or 5 feet in all directions and will need ample water and at least one feeding. The sooner you harvest the fruit, the better it will taste, but the cucumbers will grow as long as 2½ feet. Seeds for these slender, curving cucumbers are available in some nurseries and through mail-order catalogs.

Eggplant

Heat-loving relative to the tomato and pepper. Set out four plants to yield 12 eggplants in 2 to 3 months.

Top: *white*
Center: *purple*
Bottom: *midget variety*

People who wrinkle their noses at the mention of eggplant are missing the gustatory delights of one of the best meat substitutes that can be grown in the garden. Prepared in cheese, egg, and tomato casseroles or sliced, batter-dipped, and fried, eggplant can win over most doubters.

Eggplant fruits can be bitter when they pass the best harvest stage and seeds mature. Rarely, however, does a home garden produce bitter fruit, because gardeners tend to harvest eggplants before this point. Each plant should yield at least three or four fruits. Eggplants make excellent container specimens in tubs or boxes.

Eggplant is a heat-loving, frost-tender, summer vegetable. Because it sprouts and grows slowly from seeds, plants are customarily purchased. If eggplant is grown from seeds, a soil temperature of 75° is necessary for good sprouting.

Recommended varieties. 'Black Beauty' (early variety; large, dark, glossy purple fruit), 'Burpee Hybrid' (vigorous variety with large fruit; resistant to drought and disease), 'Dusky Hybrid' (early variety recommended for areas with short growing seasons), 'Early Beauty' (early variety that bears oval fruit; compact growth habit), 'Early Hybrid' (good fruit production over a longer season than most eggplants; slightly smaller fruit), 'Morden Midget' (good fruit production over a long season; slightly smaller fruit), 'White Beauty' (white fruit; decorative plant with fruit, can be used as ornamental in flower beds or containers).

How to plant. Eggplant seeds sprout slowly; set out transplants after the ground warms up and all danger of frost is past. Space the plants 3 feet apart in rows 3 to 4 feet apart. If nights turn cold, protect the plants with a covering (see page 15, 17).

Care. Feed and water these as you do peppers (see page 65). If you starve eggplant bushes or let them dry out, the fruit set will be sparse. Restrict the number of fruits on a plant to six by pinching off tip shoots and removing extra blossoms.

Pests. Colorado potato beetle can defoliate young plants. Control with rotenone, sevin, or diazinon. Eggplant lacebug, a troublesome pest in the South, feeds on the underside of leaves. Dust or spray with malathion. If aphids infest foliage, control them with rotenone or malathion (note label precautions). Wilt diseases of the same types that attack tomatoes and potatoes will sometimes affect eggplant. The only "cure" is to try to avoid it by rotating crops and not growing eggplant in places where tomatoes or potatoes have been grown in the past three years.

Harvesting. Pick when glossy, dark purple, and about 6 inches long. Use a knife or kitchen shears to snip off the fruits. Wear gloves — the stems are prickly. If some of the fruits reach full size and begin to lose their glossy sheen, don't eat them; cut off and discard the old fruit to encourage formation of new fruit.

In containers. Striking foliage, fruit, and blossoms and a worthwhile yield from a single plant make eggplant ideal for containers. Choose a tub or box with a capacity of at least 2 cubic feet.

Endive

Plant seeds of curly or broad-leafed types. Takes more heat than lettuce.

Top: *curly.* **Bottom:** *French*

If you are a salad lover, reserve a row in your late-summer garden for endive. A short row of 6 to 12 plants will give you a delicious substitute for lettuce until heavy frosts kill the plants. Endive plants are low growing and can spread to 18 inches wide.

Recommended varieties. 'Full Heart Batavian' is the smooth-leafed endive ordinarily sold as "Escarole." 'Green Curled' has deeply cut, curly leaves. Both mature in about three months from seeds; this dictates spring planting in cool, short-season areas.

How to plant. Endive is not particular about the type of soil you plant it in. Over most of the country, late summer plantings for a fall harvest are most successful. Plant seeds ¼ inch deep and 1 inch apart. In dry weather, dig a furrow 3 inches deep and scatter seeds in the bottom. Cover the seeds with 1 inch of soil and flood the furrow daily until the seeds sprout. Thin to 12 to 18 inches apart. Space rows about 24 inches apart. Although hot-weather thinnings can be bitter in taste, the flavor will improve with cool weather and blanching.

Care. If the endive flavor is a little strong for your taste, gather the outer leaves up and tie them loosely. This will blanch the hearts and make them mild and tender. The best time to blanch is two to three weeks before the harvest stage.

Pests. Endive has few insect problems, but snails and slugs can eat the foliage. Spread ashes around the plants and pick the pests off at night. Or scatter snail and slug bait around the base of plants, watering to activate the bait.

Harvesting. A single head of endive can make salads for a small family, or outer leaves can be pulled off without harming the plant. Any excess endive can be cooked. You can protect late-maturing heads against freezing by mounding up soil or straw around them (see page 24).

In containers. The curly-leafed type is the most attractive. Sow a circle of seeds in a large tub or grow one plant per 8-inch pot.

FRENCH ENDIVE

You will also see this delicacy called Belgian endive, Witloof chicory, and *radicchio*. It takes special care, and is usually expensive.

Plant seeds indoors in flats, transplanting them in the spring into rich soil that has been worked to a depth of 18 inches. Keep the soil moist and weed free. If growth is slow, apply a complete fertilizer.

In the fall, dig the mature plants carefully. Wash and trim roots to 9 inches long. Remove all the leaves except for the single central bud. The next step is forcing, which produces the pale cluster of well-blanched leaves. Place roots with buds pointing up in a 2-foot-deep bed of moist sand. Cover the roots with 6 to 10 inches of the sand kept damp and at room temperature. In 4 to 6 weeks, remove the blanched heads by pulling at the roots instead of tugging on the tender leaves. Cut the roots off before washing and serving the heads.

Herbs

Choose nursery plants or seeds of your favorites in early spring to add special flavor to your summer crops.

Left to right: *chives, rosemary, mint, parsley, dill, basil, oregano*

Tucked in the garden or growing in containers, fresh herbs provide fragrance and flavoring. Herbs include annuals, biennials, or perennials, but most of them thrive in full sun and in soil that is not too rich. (Too rich a soil dissipates their flavor.) Some of the most popular and useful herbs are listed here.

How to plant. Plant seeds of annual herbs in the ground or indoors in containers in the spring. If your soil tends toward acidity, add lime. Sow, thin, and cultivate as you would for vegetables. Nursery plants are practical if you only want a few.

Perennial herbs are usually sown in seed boxes and transplanted to flats or pots, from which they are planted into the garden. Many of them, such as rosemary and marjoram, are propagated from cuttings as well as from seeds. French tarragon does not produce seeds and can be grown from cuttings only.

Care. Herbs appreciate moderate amounts of complete fertilizer.

Harvesting and preserving. Herbs to be dried and stored should be harvested when the flavor-bearing oils are richest and most concentrated. With herbs grown for their leaves, this point is reached just as the flower buds begin to open or after the first flower has unfolded. Cut herbs early in the morning, but after any moisture on them has dried. Strip the leaves from the stem, remove flower heads, and place the leaves loosely and thinly on trays with mesh bottoms through which air can freely circulate. The room in which the leaves are dried should be warm and dry, with no direct sunlight reaching the trays. Stir the leaves each morning for four or five days or until they are completely dry; then put them in airtight containers, such as glass jars. Or hang herbs in small bundles to dry.

BASIL

Sweet basil is a bushy annual that is easy to grow. The leaves and tender tips are spicy and flowerlike in flavor and odor. A few plants can be potted in the fall and brought indoors for winter use. Use basil fresh or dried. For contrast in an herb bed, look for the variety 'Dark Opal'. Its bronze foliage tastes like the green varieties.

Culture. Basil needs sun, average moisture, and light, well-drained soil. Plant seeds each month for a steady supply of the herb. Pinch out tips and flowers to keep plants bushy. Plants will produce two large crops a year.

BAY

This is actually a mild-climate tree (sweet bay or *Laurus nobilis*), the leaves of which are used for flavoring. Leaves of the California bay can be substituted.

Culture. Buy plants from a nursery, for seeds take a long time to germinate. This tree is frequently grown in large tubs on the patio. Many gardeners keep the head clipped in a rounded form.

CHIVES

This perennial herb grows in clusters from bulbs. The tops of the leaves can be continually clipped for use as an onionlike seasoning.

Culture. Buy plants from a nursery, since plants grown from seeds take 2 years to mature. Chives need fairly rich soil, full sun, and regular fertilizer; keep the soil moist. Plants in containers can go indoors in a sunny window.

DILL

Dill is an annual whose leaves and seeds are used fresh or dried in making pickles and in flavoring salads and many other foods.

Culture. Broadcast seeds in spring after danger of frost is past. The spot should receive full sun and have good, well-drained soil. Thin the plants to 12 inches apart when they are 2 to 3 inches high. Or sow them in containers at least 10 inches deep.

Pinch off leaves to use any time after the plants are large enough to spare the foliage. Tie a small plastic bag over seed heads at maturity. When seeds begin to drop into the bag, brush remaining seeds into the bag and store.

MARJORAM

This tender plant is a perennial in mild-winter areas. Elsewhere, it's grown outdoors as an annual or indoors in containers. It is a bushy little plant about 2 feet high, with soft foliage and white flowers in knotted clusters. Use the leaves fresh or dried.

Culture. Marjoram likes full sun and fairly moist soil. Keep blossoms cut off and the plant trimmed to prevent woody growth. Propagate from seeds, cuttings, or root divisions.

MINT

There are many kinds of mint in popular use. The most common is the perennial spearmint, which grows to 2 feet tall and has dark green leaves with leafy spikes of purplish flowers. Use it fresh.

Culture. Mint takes full sun or partial shade. With adequate moisture, it spreads rapidly by underground stems. It is advisable to contain the roots in a box or pot to keep them from taking over the garden. Propagate mint from runners.

OREGANO

Also known as wild marjoram, this perennial grows to 2½ feet tall. Medium-size leaves are oval shaped; blooms are purplish pink. Although oregano is best fresh, you can also use it dried.

Culture. Oregano likes sun, medium-rich soil, good drainage, and average watering. Keep the plant trimmed to prevent flowering. Replant every 3 years.

PARSLEY

Parsley is a compact, bushy annual except in mild-winter areas where it may be perennial. Plants lend themselves to border and container plantings. They will also grow well indoors in a sunny window. Cutting the outer branches for use as a seasoning or garnish will stimulate new growth. Good varieties to grow are 'Hamburg' (produces an edible white root that resembles a parsnip), 'Moss Curled', 'Paramount' (triple-curled), 'Plain', and 'Single'.

Culture. Parsley seeds take at least 3 weeks to sprout and then they grow so slowly that weeds tend to overgrow the seedlings. Buy plants or start seeds indoors (see page 12) and transplant them after danger of heavy frost is past. Sow seeds ¼ inch deep. Set in plants or thin to about 18 inches apart. Spring-planted parsley will produce until killed by heavy fall frosts. Parsley will live through the winter in mild areas and will shoot up seed stalks when the days grow long and warm. Give parsley a light feeding with a nitrogen-rich fertilizer whenever its deep green color begins to fade. Water deeply.

ROSEMARY

This half-hardy perennial has a sweet fragrant scent, and the shrubs themselves are ornamental. Foliage is gray green; the flowers pale to dark blue depending on the variety. Shrubs reach 3 to 5 feet tall, but a spreading form is lower growing.

Culture. Rosemary requires full sun and well-drained, gravelly soil that isn't too rich. Buy plants from a nursery. The plant is drought resistant and can be propagated from cuttings.

SAGE

This is a shrubby perennial. The common form has gray green leaves with blue flowers. Other forms with the same flavor are 'Variegated Sage' with cream and purple leaf markings; and 'Golden Sage'. These varieties grow about 2 feet tall. 'Pineapple Sage' has mint green leaves with a pineapple flavor. It grows about 4½ feet tall and has vermilion flowers in late fall.

Culture. Sage likes sun and poor soil. It is fairly drought resistant. Cut the plant back after it blooms. Fertilize if you cut it continually. Divide the plants every 3 to 4 years.

Propagate sage from cuttings or grow the common variety from seed (it germinates easily).

SAVORY

There are two kinds of savory — an annual summer type and a perennial winter type. Most popular is the summer savory, an 18-inch annual that grows easily from seed. The leaves of both kinds are narrow and green and are usable fresh or dried.

Culture. Savory likes full sun, an adequate amount of moisture, and light soil. Grow summer savory from seeds; buy plants of winter savory from a nursery. Clip at the start of the flowering season for drying.

TARRAGON

There are two kinds: the marvelously fragrant and flavorful French tarragon, grown only from cuttings or divisions; and the unexciting Russian variety grown from seeds. The only way to be sure you are getting the French kind is to bruise a leaf to test for the strong fragrance. This kind grows into a perennial bush about 2 feet tall that dies back to the ground each winter.

Culture. This hardy plant thrives even in poor soil as long as it is well drained. Give it some sun and normal watering. New plants can be started easily from divisions in the spring.

THYME

There are many kinds of thyme, all perennials and easy to grow. Some kinds grow 8 to 12 inches high; others form a mat close to the ground that you can walk on. Favorite kinds are 'Silver Thyme' with a cream border around the leaves; and 'Lemon Thyme' with a yellow border and lemony thyme fragrance and flavor.

Culture. Plant thyme in sun and light, sandy soil that is moderately dry (thyme thrives in hot, dry places where most other plants fail). Prune after flowering. Replant every three years. Thyme grows well from tip cuttings taken in spring and grows easily from seeds.

To dry herbs, *hang them upside down or place stripped leaves on mesh-bottom trays.*

Horseradish

Grow in cool climates in rich, moist soil. Dig one root at a time to use when it's fresh and hot.

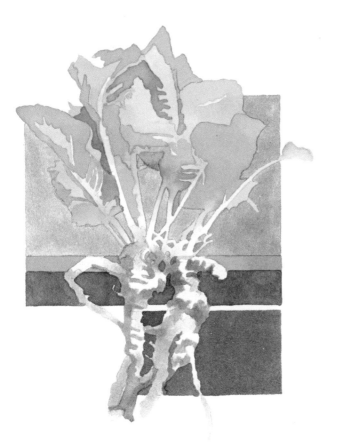

Horseradish root looks like an old dog bone. You can make horseradish sauce by peeling the root and blending it with vinegar. Grind together three parts horseradish cubes with one part white vinegar and a little salt. You can refrigerate the sauce for up to three months or freeze it.

How to plant. Buy a root at the store, stick it in the ground, and it should grow within a few weeks. It can be that easy. For more plants, buy a root with several crowns at the top end. Cut off each of these little crowns along with a wedge of the main root 2 to 3 inches long and plant them about 1 foot apart. Set the cuttings small end down and big end 2 inches below the soil surface. Plant them in a sunny place in loose, rock-free soil so the roots can grow uninhibited.

Harvesting. Roots grow most in late summer and early fall, so the best time to harvest is in October or November. From late fall through spring, dig up roots with a pitchfork as you're ready to use them. Once your plants are fully established, you can probably dig some outer roots year round. Freshly dug roots are most flavorful.

In containers. The horseradish root is too large to be practical for containers.

Jerusalem artichoke

Plant tubers of this perennial in spring or fall. Foliage dies back in winter, regrows the following spring.

These tubers are a lazy gardener's dream plant—big crop for little effort. In food markets these tubers are relatively uncommon, but in a garden they grow and multiply like weeds. The tubers may be sold as "sunchokes."

You plunk the tubers into the ground as soon as soil is workable in spring (or in late fall). When the weather gets warm, up sprout spring plants that reach 6 feet or more. Yellow flowers bloom in late summer. Around November when leaves begin to die, you dig up big clumps of tubers to eat. They are crisp and sweet. Use them cooked or raw, somewhat like water chestnuts or new potatoes.

How to plant. Plant the tubers (or chunks with 2 or 3 eyes) 10 to 18 inches apart and 2 to 4 inches deep.

Care. Jerusalem artichokes aren't fussy about poor soil or scarce water (although they do best with reasonably rich soil and regular watering) but be sure to give them full sun. Choose firm, plump tubers from a grocery store or nursery (shriveled ones don't always grow); or order tubers by mail.

Harvesting. You may dig up plants with over 10 pounds of tubers each. This is delightful as long as you keep up with the harvest. If you want to prevent them from taking over your yard, it's wise to dig up excess tubers each spring. After being harvested in the fall, tubers dry out quickly, so store them in an airtight container in the refrigerator or in a cool place embedded in moist sand or sawdust. Better yet, dig only the amount you can use at one meal. They taste best immediately after harvest.

In containers. The plant's spreading habit makes it impractical for containers.

Kohlrabi

Plant seeds of this cabbage relative in the spring garden for early summer harvest or the late summer garden for fall harvest.

Kale

Stretch the season by planting kale for harvesting during cold weather since flavor is improved by light frosts.

Top: *white*
Bottom: *purple*

Producing prodigious crops of sweet greens for cooking from summer through heavy frost, curly green kale is loaded with vitamins. The plants grow to 2 or 3 feet in height and equally as wide. If you keep such pets as guinea pigs, chickens, and rabbits, they will love fresh young kale leaves. And if you have always considered kale a "pot herb" for cooking, try tiny young leaves raw in salads. Plant kale in spring where summers are cool; plant after midsummer elsewhere. To harvest, cut off the outer leaves as needed. Pull smaller plants to thin.

For planting instructions and care see collards, page 46. Kale is subject to the same pests as cabbage; see that section for recommended controls.

Recommended varieties. 'Dwarf Blue Curled Vates' (withstands temperatures below freezing; compact shortstemmed plant), 'Dwarf Siberian' (plumelike, slightly frilled foliage).

In containers. Use large containers and just harvest the outer leaves to keep plants growing all season.

A packet of kohlrabi seeds will give you buckets of delicious "above-ground turnips" for very little work. Spring-seeded kohlrabi sprouts and grows rapidly. When the plants are 6 to 8 inches high, the stems will begin to swell just above the root line until the "bulbs" are 3 to 4 inches across. Peeled and steamed, kohlrabi has a mild flavor somewhat like turnips — but far more delicate, with a crispness like that of water chestnuts. Try thin slices sautéed in butter.

Green and purple varieties are available; both have creamy white interiors. Kohlrabi matures in about two months. Eat kohlrabi when bulbs are 2 to 3 inches in diameter; they can get stringy when overly mature.

Broadcast seeds or plant them in wide bands. Thin to 12 inches apart. The young greens from thinnings can be combined with other kinds of greens and cooked. Kohlrabi can be stored much like turnips (see page 75). Feed plants about every 3 weeks. Keep the soil moist.

Recommended varieties. 'Early Purple Vienna', 'Early White Vienna'.

In containers. Plants are unusual looking, grow rapidly, and will succeed in planters 8 to 10 inches deep.

Lettuce

Tuck seeds into any bare spot—different varieties in different spots for interesting salads.

Top: *Bibb.* **Bottom left to right:** *red leaf, iceberg, romaine*

Lettuce is one of the easiest of all vegetables to grow from seeds. There are dozens of kinds and varieties to choose from. Dedicated lettuce fanciers can search seed racks and catalogs each planting season for new varieties to brighten the family salad bowl and surprise dinner guests. You can stagger plantings for a continuous crop. There are four types of lettuce. Leaf or loosehead lettuce forms a loose head that separates into large individual leaves for salads. It matures in 40 to 45 days. Butterhead forms small, rather open and irregular heads that blanch to a creamy interior color. It matures in 65 to 80 days. Romaine has upright, cylindrical, lightly folded heads that can easily be separated into individual leaves. It matures in 70 days if summer planted — 80 if spring planted. Head lettuce requires 80 to 95 days to develop to full size.

Recommended varieties. Leaf: 'Black Seeded Simpson' (fast growing; outer leaves have a crumpled texture), 'Early Prizehead' (brownish red leaves), 'Grand Rapids' (slow to go to seed; will grow in a greenhouse in winter), 'Green Ice' (glossy dark green leaves; slow to go to seed), 'Oakleaf' (heat resistant), 'Ruby' (reddish bronze leaves), 'Salad Bowl' (slow to go to seed), 'Slo-bolt' (compact dwarf plants; slow to go to seed). Butterhead varieties: 'Bibb' (Limestone), 'Buttercrunch' (heat-resistant Bibb), 'Butter King' (disease resistant; slow to go to seed), 'Deer Tongue' (slow to go to seed), 'Fordhook', 'Great Lakes' (very productive, even under adverse conditions; resistant to tipburn and heat), 'Tom Thumb' (miniature; good in containers). Romaine (Cos) varieties: 'Paris White', 'Valmaine' (disease resistant). Head: 'Iceberg' (vigorous), 'Imperial No. 44' (forms good heads in warm weather), 'Premier Great Lakes' (resistant to tipburn and heat).

How to plant. Lettuce is a cool-weather crop — there's no doubt about it. Lettuce not only sulks and goes to seed in hot weather, but the seeds will also refuse to sprout in very warm soil. Lettuce grows readily in cool soil, so make your plantings in very early spring and at 2-week intervals until late spring. Then delay additional plantings until the weather cools off.

Quick-maturing leaf lettuce is the favorite where hot, humid summers follow closely on the heels of spring weather. In these areas, however, good crops of romaine or butterhead may be grown in fall if seeds are planted in late summer.

Spring crops of head lettuce from seeds sown indoors 4 to 6 weeks before the average frost-free date and set out as good-size plants mature ahead of the warm weather. Fall crops of all types can be grown from seeds sown directly in the garden. In the northern tier of states, high-altitude gardens, and in cool coastal climates, lettuce can be grown all summer long.

Plant seeds ¼ inch deep and 1 inch apart in rows 18 inches apart. Set plants of heading varieties no less than 12 inches apart in rows 24 inches apart. If spaced more closely, they won't form large heads.

If you experience difficulty in sprouting lettuce seeds due to dry or hot soils, place a cupful of moistened sphagnum moss in a plastic bag and add a few dozen seeds. Store the bag in the vegetable freshener of the refrigerator during the day; take it out at night. The alternating temperatures should initiate sprouting within 2 to 3 weeks. Watch the seeds carefully and as soon as they show signs of sprouting, plant them — moss and all — during the cool evening hours. Cover with ¼ inch of soil and moisten the row thoroughly and often until the seedlings are established.

Care. Give leaf lettuce only light fertilization at planting time; heading types will respond to a second light feeding when plants are half grown. Water lettuce often.

Pests. Small green worms, slugs, and snails occasionally pester lettuce. Scatter bait on the ground to keep slugs and snails away. Pick off the green worms by hand.

Harvesting. Mature lettuce plants can be pulled for harvest, giving you a mixture of large and small leaves. If you have only a few plants, pull and eat just the outer leaves without sacrificing whole plants. Use all thinnings, of course, in salads. Leaf lettuce such as 'Grand Rapids' or 'Prizehead' can be cut off an inch or two above the ground and the plants will send out new leaves for a second crop. You can harvest head lettuce when the center is firm to the touch.

In containers. Small size and fast growth make lettuce an ideal container crop. All you need is a soil depth of 6 inches and regular watering and feeding.

Melons

Summer plants with a voracious appetite for warmth, water, and space. The mouth-watering fruits take about 3 months to mature from seeds.

Top left to right: *honeydew, Crenshaw*
Bottom left to right: *watermelon, icebox watermelon, cantaloupe*

Like their fellow members of the cucurbit family (squash and cucumbers) melons thrive in warm weather and well-drained soil, take up lots of space, and need regular, ample water. If you can provide these requirements, home grown melons will reward you with a vine-ripened sweetness impossible to find in the market.

If you don't have a very long warm season, however, look for the earlier maturing hybrids that can be successful in all areas but those with the coolest or shortest summers. Compact varieties with short vines, such as 'Minnesota Midget' cantaloupe, even make it possible to grow melons in a small garden.

The silvery green to buff or golden cantaloupe (muskmelon) is the fastest maturing and easiest to grow of the melons.

The long-season melons — such as the green-skinned 'Persian', the pink-fleshed 'Crenshaw', the lime green-fleshed 'Honeydew', and the white-fleshed 'Casaba' — require up to 115 warm days to mature and dislike high humidity. They grow best in the warm interior valleys of the West and Southwest.

Watermelons — once considered long-season vegetables — can now be grown wherever cantaloupes mature reliably, thanks to new short-season varieties. The quick-maturing types called "icebox" melons have smaller fruits than those sold commercially. The large-fruited varieties require 85 to 90 days or more to ripen fully; they grow best in the southern states and in warm western interior valleys.

Recommended varieties. Cantaloupes: 'Ambrosia' (sweet fruit), 'Burpee Hybrid', 'Far North' (early variety; compact), 'Hale's Best', 'Haogen' (vigorous), 'Iroquois', 'Mainerock Hybrid' (early variety; resistant to fusarium

Left: *To keep melons from rotting on damp soil, prop them on clay pots or* (**right**) *place on boards.*

wilt), 'Minnesota Midget' (early variety; compact, vines to 3 feet, fruit to 4 inches), 'Samson Hybrid' (resistant to powdery mildew and fusarium wilt), 'Saticoy' (long season; resistant to wilt disease; tolerant of powdery mildew and fruit spot). Melons related to cantaloupe: 'Burpee Early Hybrid Crenshaw' (outer skin turns yellow green when fruit is ripe; freezes well), 'Golden Beauty Casaba' (restricted to warm climates), 'Honey Mist' (honeydew; high sugar content, will ripen in northern climates), 'Kazakh' (early honeydew), 'Persian' (restricted to warm climates).

Watermelons: 'Charleston Gray' (disease resistant), 'Crimson Sweet', 'Dixie Queen Hybrid' (vigorous; flesh has low fiber content; resistant to wilt disease), 'Fordhook Hybrid', 'Golden Midget' (early variety; good in northern climates; fruit to 8 inches; outer skin turns golden when ripe), 'Klondike', 'Lollipop' (available in yellow and red-fleshed varieties; small, very sweet fruit), 'New Hampshire Midget' (small plant and fruit; very productive), 'Peacock', 'Petite Sweet' (early variety; small fruit), 'Sugar Baby' (small sweet fruit with few seeds; has a thin rind), 'Super Sweet', 'Sweet Princess' (disease resistant), 'Triple Sweet Seedless Hybrid' (sweet seedless flesh; pollinating variety is included in seed packet), 'Yellow Baby Hybrid' (yellow, very sweet flesh; small fruit).

How to plant. Unless you live where summers are long and warm both day and night, start melon seeds indoors in late spring in peat pots, large paper cups that can be torn without disturbing the root ball, or other deep, well-drained containers. Cover seeds with 1 inch of soil; they sprout at 75°. Seedlings will grow very rapidly in a sunny spot or under fluorescent lights, so don't start them more than 2 to 3 weeks before the frost-free date. Transplant carefully; melon seedlings have few roots and are fragile. Set plants 3 to 8 feet apart, depending on variety.

Before planting seeds directly in the ground, wait until you find the soil has warmed to the 70° to 75° required to sprout seeds. Plant 1 inch deep in circles of five seeds and later thin to three plants per circle.

Melons respond dramatically to manure or fine compost in the soil and to being grown on mounds raised 6 inches above garden level for drainage and warmth. Build mounds for three plants by excavating about a bushel of soil, mixing with equal parts of organic matter and refilling the hole. Add a complete garden fertilizer when mixing the soil and feed plants every 4 to 6 weeks.

Grow melons in full sun at the side of the garden where the robust vines can be trained away from smaller vegetables. Vines are brittle and break easily, so train them while young. See page 21 for ideas on space-saving frames and supports.

Care. Mulch around the plants with straw to maintain an even level of soil temperature and moisture and to reduce loss of fruit to rotting. Watch the tips of vines for signs of wilting; then soak around the plants thoroughly. While melons are ripening, place them on boards or other low supports to prevent their rotting from contact with moist soil.

Pests. Virus-carrying insects, such as cucumber beetles, can cripple young plants. If the plants slowly turn yellow and start to dry up, pull them up and replant. Spray with diazinon when beetles appear, stopping when label instructions indicate.

Harvesting. Here are some clues to ripeness in melons: for cantaloupes, if the stem slips off easily, the melon is ripe. Also, the opposite end softens and the netting becomes thick and corky as the fruit ripens.

For Persian and Crenshaw, try the aroma test. Sniff the blossom end; if it smells sweet and fruity, the melon is ready. (Crenshaw can be fully ripe, yet have a green skin.) For honeydew and casaba, pick when the rind has turned deep yellow. The blossom end also tends to become springy instead of firm.

Even the experts are sometimes fooled by watermelons, but these tips can help you pick them at their prime. Rap the melon with your knuckles; a dull "plunk" means the watermelon is probably ready — a higher pitched "ping" means wait a few days and thump it again. (This test is most reliable in the early morning.) Also, note the two curly tendrils that extend from the stem nearest the fruit. When these turn brown, the melon is likely to be ripe. Check the light spot on the underside of the fruit. When this turns from white to light yellow, the melon is probably ready. Or, press down firmly on the top of the fruit with the palm of your hand. If you feel the flesh crack inside, it is ready to eat.

In containers. Large plants, slow growth, and low yield per plant make melons impractical for containers.

Mustard greens

Choose curly or smooth types. Plant seeds in the garden to mature during cool weather.

Plants of mustard grow knee high in 35 to 45 days and develop large, wide leaves. Cool weather improves the flavor. During hot weather the peppery tang of the greens can become strong, especially in older leaves.

Once flowering has started, it is useless to snap the tops off in the hope that new crops of leaves will form. Flowering is your signal to wait until cooler weather to plant a new batch of seeds.

Recommended varieties. 'Burpee's Fordhook Fancy' (curled leaves; slow to go to seed), 'Florida Broad Leaf' (good variety for sandy soils as the smooth leaves are easy to wash), 'Southern Giant Curled' (curled leaves with mild flavor), 'Tendergreen' (combination of spinach and mustard; fast growing; heat and drought resistant).

How to plant. Mustard seeds sprout reliably in cool soil. The plants thrive in cool weather but quickly go to seed in the heat of summer. As early in the spring as the soil can be worked, plant seeds ½ inch deep and 1 to 2 inches apart. Thin plants to stand 2 to 3 feet apart. Eat the thinnings. Plant again in late summer. In mild-winter areas, plant again in fall and winter.

Care. Fertilize lightly when seeds are planted. Water frequently and generously.

Pests. Hose off aphids and pick off cabbage worms or control them with *Bacillus thuringiensis* (note label precautions).

Harvesting. Pull plants only when thinning. Otherwise, snap off leaves, leaving the growing tip to produce replacements.

Leaves of 3 to 4 inches in length are tender enough to use in salads. Stringy stems are usually trimmed off larger leaves before the leaves are cooked.

Light frosts don't bother mustard; harvest can continue until heavy freezes wipe out the plants.

In containers. Fill boxes or pots with at least 6 inches of loose soil. Harvest outer leaves as you can use them.

Okra

If your garden will grow good sweet corn, it will grow good okra. Plant seeds when soil has warmed up.

Okra or gumbo has a slightly mucilaginous consistency that takes some getting used to. However, when dipped in batter, breaded and fried, chopped for use in soup stock or sea food gumbos, or served with black-eyed peas, young okra pods are delicious.

Okra pods grow on large, erect, bushy plants with tropical-looking leaves. The pods appear where leaf stems join the main stem.

Recommended varieties. 'Clemson Spineless' (has none of the prickles that make it necessary to wear gloves when harvesting other varieties), 'Dwarf Long Pod' (short plants to 2½ feet), 'Perkins', 'Red Okra' (tall plants to 6 feet; pods are bright red, turn green when cooked; dried pods can be used in floral arrangements).

How to plant. Okra seeds need a soil temperature of 70° to 75° to sprout. Sprouting can be improved by soaking seeds in water for 24 hours before planting. Sow seeds in groups of three in a sunny, well-drained area at the back of the garden where the large plants won't shade smaller vegetables. Mature plants should stand 3 feet apart.

Care. Okra plants are very heat resistant but need lots of water and fairly fertile soil (fertilize at least once during the growing season). Plants yield late and poorly where summers are cool. Elsewhere, late-spring planting will begin yielding in midsummer and continue until a killing frost. Eight to twelve plants should yield enough pods to feed four people.

Pests. Okra is troubled by few pests, but borers occasionally necessitate preventive sprays of sevin (note label precautions).

Harvesting. Pods should be harvested with a paring knife when they're 1 to 3 inches in length; they can get tough if allowed to go more than a day or two past their prime. Remove overripe pods to maintain vigor in plants.

In containers. The variety 'Red River' has a tropical look and in a large tub on a warm patio would yield enough okra to make one plant worth growing. Other varieties are too tall and rangy looking to be decorative.

Onion family

All members of the onion family dislike temperature extremes. Plant tiny onions called "sets" for a head start on the harvest date.

Top left to right: *garlic, white, red, leek.* **Bottom left to right:** *bunching or scallions, yellow*

Onions may be easily grown from seeds, started plants, or "sets." If you want lots of green onions (scallions) or large, sweet, mild-flavored bulbs at low cost, start from seeds. In short-season areas, started plants of the mild Bermuda or sweet Spanish onions can bring in an earlier bulb harvest.

"Sets" are small bulbs of special varieties of onions. When you plant these tiny bulbs, the outer flesh sloughs off as new green scallions rise from the center of the bulb. Let them grow on from spring planting and they will form medium-size, rather strong-flavored bulbs for summer harvest.

Recommended varieties. True bunching, non-bulbing types for scallions are 'Beltsville Bunching', 'Evergreen Bunching' (sow seeds in spring or summer for fall harvest). Spring-planted varieties for bulbs are 'Autumn Spice', 'Early Yellow Globe' (large onion with mild flavor), 'Ebenezer' (flat bulbs with mild flavor; stores well), 'Fiesta Hybrid', 'Southport Red Globe' (strong flavor), 'South-

New seedlings *form on mature leek; plant 3 to 4 inches apart.*

port Yellow Globe' (strong flavor), 'Sweet Spanish' (extra large bulbs with mild flavor). Fall-planted varieties for mild-winter areas are 'Bermuda' (yellow, red, and white; flat bulbs with mild flavor), 'Crystal White Wax' (mild flavor; popular in southern areas where it develops a large bulb), 'Early Harvest No. 5 Hybrid', 'Granex' (large flat bulb with mild flavor), 'Grano', 'Italian Long Red' or 'Torpedo'.

The varieties indicated for spring planting form bulbs only on shortening autumn days. Varieties for fall planting in mild climates form bulbs only during the lengthening days of spring.

How to plant. Onion family members like cool weather. Seeds sprout best in cool soil. Plant seeds ¼ inch deep and rather thickly; pull and transplant or eat the excess scallions as you thin. Plants should stand about 4 inches apart for bulb formation — 1 to 2 inches apart for scallions. Sets or plants should be planted 2 inches deep. Space rows about 12 to 18 inches apart.

Care. Onion family members have rather small root systems and need fairly frequent applications of fertilizer in order to form large bulbs. In heavy soil, grow them in raised beds for good drainage but keep the soil moist at all times to maintain steady growth. It is essential for good bulb formation to keep onions weeded, but roots are shallow and easily damaged by deep cultivation. Hand-pull weeds or scrape the surface with a scuffle hoe.

Harvesting. Pull bunching onions or thin bulbing onions as soon as the scallions are big enough to make it worth the effort. Bulbing onions, garlic, and shallots must be completely dry to store well. When about half the tops have lopped over, break over the rest to hasten maturity. Dig up the bulbs and sun-dry them, making sure they are not bruised or soaked by rain showers and that the roots are completely out of the ground. (Roots covered with soil will continue to grow and the bulbs will become soft.)

In containers. The most popular members of the onion family for containers are green scallions and chives.

GARLIC

Plant the small bulb divisions or scales called "cloves" in the spring and in mild-winter areas also in October through December. Plant individual cloves with fat base downward 1 to 1½ inches deep and 2 to 3 inches apart in rows 12 inches apart. You'll have good-size bulbs in 90 days. To store, hang and dry.

LEEKS

Grow these mild-flavored, mammoth, scallionlike plants from seeds planted in early spring. In hot climates, sow seeds in summer for winter harvests. Leeks can take as long as seven months to mature from seeds, and they dislike temperature extremes — these factors give them a reputation for being difficult in many areas.

In mild-winter areas, sow between August and mid-September. Elsewhere, sow as early as possible in spring.

Sow seeds directly in furrows or transplant from containers when about 4 inches tall. Transplant or thin to 3 to 4 inches apart. Space rows 6 to 12 inches apart. Plant in full sun near the coast or during cool weather; provide partial shade during hot weather.

As leeks grow, gradually mound loose soil around the stalks to blanch them, keeping the soil surface below the leaf joints so dirt doesn't work into the bulb end.

Harvest when leeks are from ½ to 2 inches in diameter.

Lift with a garden fork in heavy soil or root tips may break off.

SHALLOTS

This small, onionlike plant produces a cluster of edible bulbs from a single bulb. The bulbs are prized in cooking for their distinct flavor.

Plant nursery plants, sets (small dry bulbs) from a seed store, or the bulbs you can buy in a grocery store. Do the planting in fall in mild climates, early spring in cold-winter areas. Place in the ground so that the bulb tips are just covered; follow procedure for planting garlic.

At maturity, tops yellow and die. Harvest by pulling clumps and separating the bulbs. Let outer skin dry for about a month before using. You can store shallots for as long as 6 months.

Parsnips

Long roots need loose, deeply worked soil. Long growing period takes patience.

Culture of this root crop is much the same as for carrots and beets, but parsnips take much longer to mature from seed — about four months. Parsnips are a cool-weather crop; the roots are quite sweet after frost has intensified the sugar. In cold-winter areas, plant seeds in late spring, let them grow through summer, harvest them in fall, and leave the excess in the ground to be dug as needed all winter. In mild-climate areas, sow seeds in fall and har-

vest in spring. Soak parsnip seeds in water 24 hours before planting to improve germination.

Recommended varieties. 'All American', 'Harris Model', 'Hollow Crown Improved'.

How to plant. Prepare the soil deeply before planting, for some varieties are 15 inches long. Sow seeds ½ inch deep in rows 3 feet apart; thin to 6 inches apart.

Care. Follow the techniques for carrots and beets.

Pests. Parsnips are remarkably free from insects and diseases.

Harvesting. Pull parsnips before the tops begin to flower. Never leave parsnips in the ground past maturity, even in winter, for they will become tough and woody. Once picked, parsnips will keep for months in cool storage.

In containers. Roots are too large to make container growing practical.

Peas

The sweetest garden peas are produced during a long season of cool weather.

Only in areas that enjoy a fairly long period of cool weather do peas yield enough to justify the space occupied. Yet the taste of fresh garden or "English" peas is so mouth-watering that most gardeners will find the space for at least a short row.

The length of row you plant depends on the variety and your climate. Where summers are quite cool or where mild winters with only light frosts provide 3 months or more of growing weather, the heavy-yielding, large-podded, tall or "pole" varieties may be grown. Elsewhere, the faster-maturing but lower-yielding "dwarf" varieties are more satisfactory. Their compact plants don't require staking or stringing. Three or four people can keep up with the output of a 10-foot row of tall peas or 20 feet of a dwarf variety.

Recommended varieties. Tall varieties: 'Alderman' (plants are 4½ to 6 feet tall; very productive), 'Green Arrow' (plants are 24 to 30 inches tall; very productive with pods concentrated at the top of the plants for easy harvesting; resistant to fusarium wilt and downy mildew). Medium-size and dwarf varieties: 'Alaska' (often planted in the Southeast because its smooth seeds don't rot in cool soils as readily as the seeds of the wrinkle-seeded types), 'Free-zonian' (very productive; fusarium wilt resistant; freezes well), 'Little Marvel' (plants only reach 18 inches in height), 'Morse's Progress No. 9', 'Wando' (heat resistant). Edible pod/sugar pea varieties: 'Dwarf Gray Sugar' (good in small gardens; short growing season), 'Giant Melting Sugar' (tall variety, to 4 feet; resistant to fusarium wilt).

How to plant. Where winters are mild, plant seeds in early fall so the plants will bear by midspring. Plant a second crop of a fast-maturing variety as early in the spring as the soil can be worked. Elsewhere, sow seeds as soon as the frost is out of the ground. Prepare the soil in the fall to permit earlier planting.

Sow seeds 1 inch deep in heavy soil, 2 inches in light soil, and 2 inches apart. For maximum use of space, peas can be planted in double rows 3 inches apart; double rows are spaced 1½ to 2 feet apart. For the tall varieties that need some support, plant double rows 6 inches apart, and leave 3 feet between each double row. If you are growing peas or beans in your garden for the first time, order a small packet of an "inoculant" from a seed catalog. This provides a special kind of soil bacteria that supplies peas with nitrogen for better growth.

Buy seeds already treated with fungicide when possible. In cool soil, at least half of the untreated pea seeds you plant will rot if a prolonged wet, cold spell arrives soon after planting. Raising the level of beds 6 inches above the surrounding soil will improve drainage and reduce rotting of seeds.

Care. For tall varieties, provide sturdy, 5-foot posts with wire stringers laced with twine. Tall peas do not twine but cling weakly and will need frequent tying up.

Peas, like beans, won't thrive in acid soil. (See page 10 for liming directions.) Go easy on adding compost and don't mulch peas; mulching keeps soil moisture at a high level and the soil cooler than is best for peas. Work in a light application of low-nitrogen fertilizer when preparing beds; you can reapply 30 days later by watering-in fertilizer.

Water peas with a soaker or through irrigation furrows. Overhead watering encourages mildew.

Toward the season's end, plants tend to mildew despite careful watering. You can retard it by dusting with sulfur.

Pests. Control pea aphids and weevils with diazinon (note label precautions).

Harvesting. Begin harvesting when pods have swelled to almost a round shape and pick them every few days. Don't let any overly mature pods remain on the plants; they reduce the total yield. Always grasp the pea vines with your free hand when pulling peas to prevent damage to the brittle vines. Pick sugar peas (edible-podded or Chinese) when pods are 2 to 3 inches long and while the seeds are still undeveloped.

In containers. Deep roots, a need for even moisture, and the number of plants required make peas an impractical container choice.

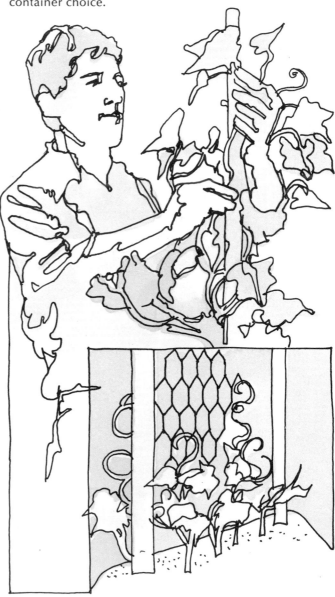

Top: *Pea vines cling weakly to support system; tie them up with string.* **Bottom:** *Plant double row around each support.*

Peppers

Pick your "snappiness" quotient from mildly pungent to eye-watering. Set out plants in warm weather.

Left to right: *yellow (hot), yellow (sweet), green (sweet), red (sweet), green (hot), red (hot)*

Dozens of varieties are available within the two major types of peppers: sweet (or bell) and hot. If a pepper is even mildly pungent, it is classed as hot. Fruits of most pepper varieties are green when young and red at maturity but are delicious at all stages. Some varieties are yellowish green to bright yellow when ripe.

Sweet peppers grow on stiff, rather compact, large-leafed bushes about 16 inches high. True hot pepper plants are taller, more spreading, and have smaller, narrower leaves. Sweet peppers mature in 65 to 80 days and can be grown anywhere in the country except in high elevations or extreme northern areas. Hot peppers ripen later and are better suited to areas with long, warm seasons, but they can be grown in northern states.

Recommended varieties. Sweet varieties: 'Bell Boy Hybrid' (resistant to tobacco mosaic; fruit red when mature), 'California Wonder' (good for stuffing), 'Canape' (hybrid), 'Golden Bell Hybrid' (early yellow-fruited variety; compact plant), 'Golden Calwonder' (golden yellow fruit), 'Keystone Giant', 'New Ace Hybrid' (productive under adverse conditions; fruit good for stuffing, freezing), 'Peter Piper' (early hybrid; very productive; resistant to tobacco mosaic), 'Pimento', 'Sweet Banana' (fruit red when mature; compact plants; very productive), 'Vinette' (miniature), 'Yolo Wonder' (resistant to tobacco mosaic; good for stuffing). Hot varieties: 'Anaheim M' (use fruit fresh or dried), 'Cayenne', 'Chili Jalapeño' (very hot), 'Hungarian Wax' (yellow fruit turns red when mature), 'Red Chili', 'Rumanian Hot', 'Tabasco'.

How to plant. Peppers are slow to start from seeds; about 8 weeks are required to grow your own to transplant stage. If you start from seeds, plant them ⅛ inch deep and sprout at a steady temperature of 70° to 80° day and night. Transplant in early summer after frost danger has passed. Set plants 2 feet apart and no deeper than they grew in the flat. Leave 2 to 3 feet between rows.

Care. Peppers should be fed every 30 to 45 days with a complete fertilizer. Too much nitrogen can cause rank growth and a poor set of blossoms. For maximum continued yields, water once or twice weekly; dry soil can inhibit fruit formation.

Plastic film mulch *covers roots of pepper to warm soil and speed root growth; also good for tomato and eggplant seedlings.*

Pests. Few bugs bother peppers, but aphids can transmit viruses from plant to plant. If any plants become stunted or mottled from the mosaic virus, pull the plants out before the virus spreads. There is no practical way to save infected plants.

Harvesting. Clip off peppers as soon as they are a usable size or when they turn to their mature color. Leaving overripe peppers on the vines can reduce yields by draining food reserves. When growing hot peppers for dry storage, let them turn red before picking. Don't rub your eyes if you have been picking hot peppers; the juice is irritating. You might wear gloves if you have quite a few to pick.

In containers. Compact plants, decorative fruits, and sustained, heavy yield make peppers ideal for containers. Provide ¾ to 1 cubic foot of soil per plant.

Potatoes

Plant seed pieces or "eyes" in early spring—be prepared for space demand and requirement for well-drained soil. This crop thrives in cool temperatures and in fertile well-drained soil.

Top: *baking*
Center: *sweet*
Bottom: *red*

You need a good-size sunny plot to grow potatoes. Vines grow about 2 feet high and are very leafy; the potato tubers form underground.

Potato vines rarely form seeds; garden potatoes are grown from seed pieces or "eyes," which are chunky segments cut from certified, disease-free tubers. Sprouts grow from the eyes, so each set should have at least two eyes. Upper portions of the sprout become tops; lower portions form roots and short stems. Sets are hard to find in most localities but can be ordered from one of the mail-order seed companies. Potatoes from produce racks are often treated with a sprout inhibitor and won't grow properly if cut up for sets.

Recommended varieties. 'Bake King' (white), 'Irish Cobbler', 'Kennebec', 'Norland' (early red).

How to plant. Very early spring planting is required except where winters are mild. In such areas crops can be planted in July for a late fall harvest.

Potatoes need a sandy, fast-draining soil; tubers become deformed in heavy, poorly drained soil. If your soil is heavy, use the following method for planting. (In any case, do not plant if soil is very wet.) Remove 2 to 3 inches of soil from the row, setting it aside. Spade deeply and fertilize. Soak the soil deeply; then let it dry for 2 to 3 days. Make a 3-inch layer of compost or spoiled hay down the length of the row. Lay the eyes 12 to 18 inches apart, the cut side down on the organic matter. Cover with another 3 inches of garden soil to keep the rough material from blowing. Large, clean tubers will form on underground stems within the warm, decomposing layer, simplifying harvesting.

Care. Because the layer of organic matter will interfere with capillary moisture flow from below, you will need to lay a soaker upside down on the row and water thoroughly every 2 to 3 weeks in dry weather. If you grow potatoes without the organic matter, apply water through irrigation furrows to avoid wetting the foliage. Knobby potatoes result if the soil dries out (stopping growth) and is wetted again.

Pests. Name almost any beetle, borer, leafhopper or caterpillar — potato vines will attract them, along with blights, leaf fungi, and tuber scab. Consult your farm advisor on the best preventive materials for your area and for the timing of controls.

Harvesting. Dig up early varieties when flowers form on the plants; on later varieties, yellowing and dying of vines will indicate the tubers have reached full size. Loosen the soil with a spading fork along the outer edges of the bed. Probe carefully so you don't impale tubers. Then, slide the spading fork under the central plant, lifting and shaking gently to remove tubers. Turn the loose soil over to find the small tubers that escaped the lifting. Don't bruise tubers or let them stand in the sun. Store them in a cool, dark area, unwashed, until ready for use. Well-matured potatoes free of defects store best.

In containers. Wide-spreading root system makes the potato a poor candidate for container growing.

SWEET POTATOES

This plant of tropical origin likes long, hot summers. Sweet potatoes also demand lots of space and well-drained soil, preferably sandy loam.

Start sweet potatoes from nursery plants or from slips. To get slips, plant the whole tuber of the variety you like in water or in sand. Use toothpicks to suspend them in water if you are just planting a few. Otherwise, plant the tubers in a deep bed of sand kept at a temperature of 70° to 75° in a hotbed or coldframe. When sprouts reach 9 inches, cut them off and plant these slips in sandy soil. Allow at least 1 foot between plants. Vines will spread 6 feet or more across.

Water frequently but don't feed with too much nitrogen or you will find all vine and no potatoes. Normal vine growth is usually lush enough to overpower weeds. Cover newly planted slips if the temperature dips.

In the fall before frost arrives, dig the tubers, being careful not to bruise the roots. If you are going to store the potatoes, don't wash them. Dry them at 80° to 85° for 2 or 3 weeks before storing them for the winter; store them at 50° to 55° F.

Recommended varieties. Dry flesh: 'Jersey Orange', 'Nemagold', 'Nugget'. Moist flesh: 'Centennial', 'Goldrush', 'Vineless Puerto Rico' (bush type without runners).

Pumpkins

Choose small varieties for pie or big ones for the thrill of watching them grow into jack-o-lantern candidates. Plant seeds in the garden when the weather has warmed.

You can grow pumpkins for cooking, canning, edible seeds, Halloween decorations, or just for the fun of it.

Varieties range in size from tiny jack-o-lanterns to giants weighing more than 100 pounds.

Planting a pumpkin vine in a small garden is analogous to letting a camel put his nose in your tent. The first thing you know, the rampant running vines will have taken over. Even the newer "bush" types spread over 20 square feet in rich soil.

Recommended varieties: Bush type (95-day maturity, 7-lb. fruits): 'Cinderella' (10-inch pumpkins), 'Spirit' (early variety). Vining (110 days to maturity, 10 to 20-lb. fruits): 'Big Tom' (fruit up to 18 lbs.), 'Jack-O-Lantern' (bright orange color), 'Lady Godiva' (hull-less seeds are excellent for roasting), 'Small Sugar' (stores well; 7-inch fruit). Mammoth type (120 days to maturity; fruits up to 100 lbs. or more): 'Big Max' (huge pumpkins up to 70 inches), 'Hungarian' (gray).

How to plant. Start pumpkins from seeds sown in the garden in early summer. Little is to be gained by starting seeds indoors because transplanting sets them back. Plant seeds in circles of three on mounds raised slightly for drainage and warmth. Space the groups of vining varieties 10 feet apart; the bush varieties need 4 to 5 feet.

Care. Feed plants twice with a balanced fertilizer before the vines spread too thickly for the fertilizer to reach the roots.

There are many theories on how to grow mammoth pumpkins. One effective way is to plant the seeds (or seedlings started in peat pots) on top of a heap of well-rotted compost. Water the vines when you see the slightest sign of wilting and feed heavily every 10 to 14 days with a dilute solution of plant food or manure water. Pinch off all but one or two pumpkins per vine. While the pumpkins are still small, lay them on wide squares of plywood to keep snails, slugs, or gophers from burrowing into the fruit.

Another good way to grow big pumpkins is to scoop a hole 4 inches deep the length of the seedbed and fill with a shovelful of manure. Cover with enough soil to bring the bed up to ground level and plant the seeds in this soil. Water, feed, and pinch off as described above.

Pests. Vine borers can be a major pest but are hard to kill with sprays. Look for holes with yellowish material coming out and slit the stalks at those places with a razor blade to remove the borers. Then heap a shovel of soil over the injured area. If the vines are vigorous, they will set roots at that point and outgrow the damage. Late-season mildew is almost unavoidable. The best preventive is to plant pumpkins where they get plenty of air movement and no overhead sprinkling.

Harvesting. Be careful not to handle green pumpkins more than necessary, for they bruise easily. When the pumpkin is ready, the skin color darkens, the skin becomes tough, and the vines dry up. Cut off pumpkins before a heavy frost comes, leaving 3 to 4 inches of stem on the fruit. If just a light frost is expected, a straw covering piled on top of the fruit is usually sufficient protection. Don't wash the fruits before storing. Store them in a warm, dry place.

In containers. Huge plants disqualify pumpkins from growing in all but the most giant containers.

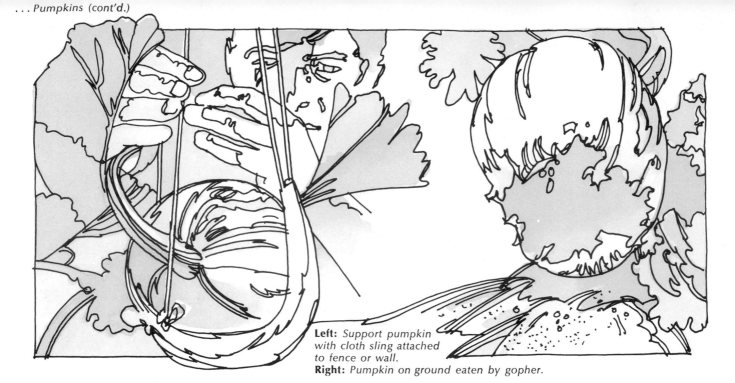

Left: *Support pumpkin with cloth sling attached to fence or wall.*
Right: *Pumpkin on ground eaten by gopher.*

Radishes

Sow seeds here and there—harvest radishes in as little as 3 weeks. Avoid hot weather harvests.

Left to right: *white, red and white, red*

Easy and fast to grow, radishes are not usually planted in special rows. Sow a pinch of radish seeds at a time here and there among slow-sprouting seeds of other vegetables or in unused corners. You might try mixing radish seeds with carrots, parsnips, or parsley if your soil is likely to form a crust. The vigorous radish seedlings will break through and open the way for the weaker seeds that might not otherwise make it. Within 3½ to 4 weeks of planting, the radishes will have matured and can be pulled. A packet of seeds will usually yield several dozen radishes.

Recommended varieties. Radish varieties differ in color, shape, mildness of flavor, and speed of maturity. Early, fast-growing varieties for spring sowing are 'Burpee White' (white roots; round when young, maturing to a flat shape), 'Champion' (round scarlet roots), 'Cherry Belle' (round red roots), 'Crimson Giant' (round red roots that grow large without becoming pithy), 'French Breakfast' (red roots with white tips; oblong shape), 'Sparkler' (round roots and scarlet tops, white bottoms), 'White Icicle' (white long roots to 5 inches; looks just like name). Summer radishes are slow growing but stand up better to hot weather: 'All Seasons' (long white roots; can be left in ground up to 6 weeks without becoming pithy), 'White Strassburg'. Large late-maturing "winter radishes" can be planted in late summer in mild climates for winter harvests: 'Long Black Spanish' (black-skinned roots), 'Sakurajima', 'White Chinese' or 'Celestial' (white roots up to 8 inches long; least pungent of the white radishes).

How to plant. Radishes are frost hardy. Sow seeds as soon as the soil can be worked in the spring and at 2-week intervals thereafter except during the hottest part of summer. Summer-grown roots turn pithy rapidly, or plants shoot to seed. Work in a light application of balanced fertilizer, plant seeds ½ inch deep and 1 inch apart, and water weekly. Space rows about 4 inches apart.

Pests. If you have had problems with grubs (maggots) boring into the roots, apply diazinon right in the furrow when you sow the seed, following label directions carefully. Any spraying after that should be done before the roots have started to swell. Summer-grown radishes are the most susceptible. Leaf miners can disfigure the leaves, but this has little effect on the roots.

Harvesting. Begin pulling radishes when they are a little larger than a pea. Pull out and discard plants as soon as roots begin to get pithy or pungent.

In containers. A soil depth of only 4 to 8 inches is needed for this fast-growing crop.

Rhubarb

Start harvesting a year after planting roots or transplants. Bushy plant is productive for at least 8 years. Partial shade or sun.

The beauty of this perennial has been its salvation in the home garden because, in most areas, its harvest season is rather short to justify the care and space it needs for an entire season. The broad, pink-tinged, crumpled leaves on tall, red, smooth stalks make interesting focal points in flower beds or in tubs. Six to eight plants of this massive, hardy perennial will keep you in rhubarb pies throughout the spring.

Rhubarb dies back or goes dormant each fall and shoots up new leaves in the spring. The plant needs a dormant period and doesn't do well in the Southeast, along the Gulf Coast, and in parts of the Southwest where winters are warm. In mild-winter areas summer dormancy can be achieved by cutting back on water for several weeks after the plant has stopped producing stalks.

Recommended varieties. 'Victoria' is available in seeds. Better varieties, such as 'Cherry', 'MacDonald', 'Strawberry', 'Valentine', are available in roots or plants.

How to plant. Prepare the soil 12 inches deep, mixing in generous amounts of compost, well-rotted manure, or other organic matter. Sow seeds, or set out plants or roots in late spring. Seed in rows about 18 inches apart, thinning plants to 12 inches apart. Plantings from seed require 2 years for initial harvest. Space plants or roots 3 to 6 feet apart. The first heavy harvest can be made the third year.

Care. Feed rhubarb plants in the early spring and again in early fall with a complete fertilizer. In areas where the soil freezes deeply, mulch rhubarb in winter after the soil has frozen. Apply 3 to 4 inches of compost or manure (not leaves) to prevent the soil from heaving and to add humus. Rhubarb is deep rooted; water plants every 2 to 3 weeks by soaking the soil deeply around the crowns.

Pests. Rhubarb has few pests.

Harvesting. Give clumps a year to become established before harvesting (rhubarb sown from seeds needs 2 years). Using a sideways twist, snap off stems at the base when they reach 12 to 18 inches in length. Trim off and discard all of the leaf blades; they are mildly poisonous. Leave a few stalks on each plant to manufacture food and rebuild the energy in the crown.

Top: *Bottomless bushel basket keeps stalks off ground.*
Bottom: *To harvest, snap off stalks with quick twist.*

In containers. Rhubarb makes a handsome container plant in a minimum of 3 cubic feet of soil per plant. If frost hits, move the container into a cool garage or cellar.

Salsify

Sow seeds in early spring. Wait up to 5 months to harvest the long, whitish roots.

The distinctive flavor of the salsify root has earned it the name "oyster plant." It looks much like a parsnip, however, and takes a long time to mature from seed like a parsnip — up to 150 days. A bed 8 feet by 3 feet will support about 30 large roots in two rows.

Recommended variety. 'Sandwich Island Mammoth' is the popular favorite.

How to plant. Since salsify is a long-season crop, it should be intercropped with something fast, such as lettuce, spinach, radishes, or Swiss chard. Work the soil to a depth of at least 18 inches so that it will be loose and crumbly. Sow the seed in rows 15 inches apart, covering them with ½ inch of fine soil. When plants are about 2 inches high, thin them out to 3 inches apart.

Care. Follow instructions for carrots and beets.

Pests. Salsify is seldom bothered by pests or diseases.

Harvesting. Don't pull the roots out of the ground too forcibly, or you'll break them. Roots can be harvested in the fall or stored in the ground all winter for a spring harvest.

In containers. Roots are too large to make container growing practical.

Spinach

This leafy crop just can't take long days and hot temperatures. Plant seeds right after frost for spring harvest or in late summer for fall harvest.

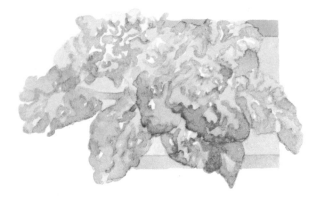

Fast-growing, short-lived spinach will mature its leafy plants in 7 weeks; then it quickly goes to seed. Plant short rows every 2 to 3 weeks to maintain a supply. Spinach definitely prefers cool weather and needs to be grown rapidly to form large, meaty leaves.

Recommended varieties. 'America' (very productive; slow to go to seed), 'Bloomsdale Long Standing' (very productive; slow to go to seed), 'Hybrid Spinach No. 7' (upright growth habit; resistant to downy mildew; good for canning and freezing), 'Hybrid Spinach No. 8' (upright growth habit; resistant to mosaic virus and blue mold), 'Melody' (large plants; resistant to downy mildew and mosaic virus), 'Nobel', 'Winter Bloomsdale' (hardy variety; slow to go to seed; blight resistant).

New Zealand spinach, which forms short runners, resembles regular spinach in leaf shape but tolerates warm weather much better. It is not a true spinach but will be productive spring and summer and is delicious raw in salads or cooked.

How to plant. Plant spinach seeds very early in the spring and periodically through early fall except during the hottest days. Plant New Zealand spinach in late spring. Sow seeds ½ inch deep. Thin to 8 inches apart; use the thinnings for salads.

Care. Nitrate forms of nitrogen fertilizer release more readily in cool weather and will help to produce good early spring, late fall, or winter crops of spinach.

Pests. Leaf miners and aphids frequently attack spinach. Hose aphids off or try washing the leaves with a soap and water solution (see page 22).

Harvesting. Nip off the outer leaves; discard the stems if they are stringy. Leave the center sprouts to form new leaves. When you first see flower buds forming in the center of the plant, quickly harvest the entire crop and use it rather than letting the spinach set seeds and be wasted.

In containers. A good crop for boxes or pots. New Zealand spinach is particularly suited to containers because it grows back quickly after cutting. Grow one plant of the New Zealand variety per 2-gallon container. Soil depth should be approximately 8 to 12 inches for regular spinach.

Squash

Once the weather warms, expect prolific growth and high yields of summer squash, large fruits on winter squash.

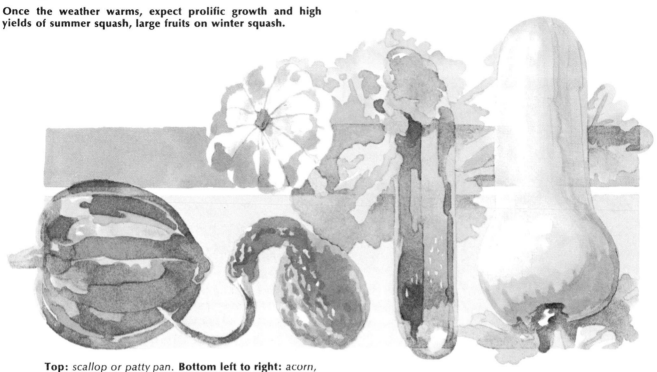

Top: *scallop or patty pan.* **Bottom left to right:** *acorn, crookneck, zucchini, butternut*

You will find two types of squash. Summer squash, the faster growing, smaller fruited type, is planted for warm-weather harvest and eaten when young—skins, immature seeds, and all. Winter squash is planted and grown just like pumpkins, which it resembles in vine size and fruiting characteristics. Summer squash can yield prodigious crops from just a few plants and will continue bearing for several weeks. The bushes are large — 2½ feet by 4 feet across at maturity — and will overgrow smaller vegetables unless given plenty of room. Winter squash, a rampant grower with bigger fruits, is grown for late harvest and winter storage. The skin is hard and inedible. Scoop out seeds and pulp before baking. Seeds may be saved, dried, and roasted.

Recommended summer varieties. Green zucchini types are 'Aristocrat' (dark green fruit borne upright on bush plants), 'Burpee Hybrid' (very productive; compact bush plants; best eaten when fruits are 6 to 8 inches long), 'Cocozelle Bush' (dark green, cylindrical fruits have lighter striping; harvest when fruits are 6 to 8 inches long). Seed packets of zucchini are sometimes labeled simply "Black" or "Green." Yellow types are 'Burpee Golden Zucchini' (bright golden cylindrical fruits with a distinct

flavor), 'Early Golden Summer Crookneck' (fruits have curved necks; harvest when fruits are 4 inches; freezes well), 'Early Prolific Straightneck' (bush plant; very productive), 'Seneca Butterbar Hybrid' (straight-necked fruits; open growth habit for easy harvesting), 'Yellow Summer Crookneck'. Patty pan or scallop types are 'Early White Bush', 'St. Pat Hybrid', 'White Bush Scallop'. 'Scallopini' is a new type of summer squash with the shape of a patty pan type and the deep green color of a zucchini that grows in bush form.

Recommended winter varieties. Bush types are 'Bush Ebony', 'Bush Table Queen', 'Kindred', 'Table King' (acorn squash). Vining or running types are 'Banana', 'Butternut' (bottle-shaped fruits; stores well), 'Golden Nugget', 'Green Cushaw', 'Hubbard' (stores well), 'Waltham Butternut' (stores well).

'Turk's Turban Ornamental Squash' can be grown for use as fall and winter decorations. The fruits are flat with a buttonlike texture; they are distinctly spotted and striped wih scarlet, orange, cream white, and green.

How to plant. Wait until frost danger is past and the soil is warm. Plant seeds 1 inch deep in circles of three to five, on hills or mounds spaced 4 to 5 feet apart. Later thin to three plants per circle (see page 15). The hills are raised about 4 inches to increase soil temperature and improve drainage.

Care. Since squash loses lots of water through its large leaves, water heavily and frequently. Mulches help conserve moisture and decrease loss of fruit to rotting (see page 20).

Squash needs plenty of fertilizer to replace the nutrients removed by heavy growth and prolific fruit production. Dry fertilizers are hard to apply because of the heavy foliage canopy. Feeding and watering can be accomplished at the same time by planting seeds around a 2 to 3-gallon can that has been perforated and sunk into the ground. Fill it full of water twice weekly and with a dilute solution of fertilizer at least once a month.

Pests. Squash vine borer can be serious, particularly east of the Rockies. (For control, see pages 22–23.) Squash bugs are difficult to control. The best method is to hand pick and destroy both the bugs and the leaves that contain the eggs. Also, remove all debris that would give winter shelter. Mildew is usually heavy in late fall; to reduce it, avoid overhead watering.

Harvesting. Pick yellow varieties when pale yellow rather than golden. Harvest scalloped squash when they are small and greenish, and before they turn white.

Summer squash should be picked before the skin turns hard; test it with your thumbnail for tenderness. From 4 to 8 inches long is the best harvest stage; the seeds and skin begin to get hard and tough in larger fruits. To prolong the harvest period, pick frequently and do not allow any fruit to reach large size.

Harvest winter squash in late fall after the vines have dried but before a heavy frost. The skin of fruits should be hard when tested with your thumbnail. Stems are thick; cut them with a sharp knife, leaving a 2-inch stub. Store the squash in a warm, dry place.

In containers. Squash plants are too big for all but the largest containers.

SPAGHETTI SQUASH

This squash looks like any other winter squash, but the flesh is made up of long, spaghetti-size strands. You can bake the whole squash and then serve the insides with just butter or any sauce that goes on spaghetti.

Plant seeds or started plants in spring in a sunny spot. Plants should be 5 to 8 feet apart. Vines will start bearing fruit in about 90 days. A handful of fertilizer in the soil will get them off to a good start.

A squash is ready to pick when the skin turns golden yellow; they will grow to between 4 and 6 pounds.

Left: *Cooked spaghetti squash is baked like regular winter squash; flesh resembles spaghetti noodles.*
Right: *Bottomless quart or gallon can provides watering basin for squash seedlings.*

Tomatoes

Harvest juicy tomatoes in as little as 2 months of warm weather after setting out plants.

Top left to right: *yellow pear, red pear, red plum.* **Bottom left to right:** *red cherry, beefsteak, yellow*

King of the vegetable garden, the tomato outranks all others in popularity. Tomatoes reward gardeners handsomely for their small investment of time and space.

Recommended varieties. Varieties differ in size of plant; in size, shape, color, and taste of fruit; and in their adaptability to different climates. Plants sold at nurseries are usually the best ones for the local climate.

Some tomato varieties were developed to grow and bear in soil that is infested with organisms that can otherwise be fatal to tomato plants — verticillium wilt, fusarium wilt, and nematodes. The variety names and seed packages either say so or they carry the letters V, F, or N after the variety name to indicate resistance to any or all of these troubles.

Cherry types are 'Burpee's Pixie Hybrid' (dwarf plant; good in containers), 'Red Cherry' (large plant; tomatoes to 1 inch), 'Small Fry Hybrid' (VFN; good in hanging baskets), 'Sweet 100' (sets up to 100 fruits on a branch; tomatoes have a very sweet flavor), 'Tiny Tim' (dwarf plant; good in containers; fruit to ¾ inch).

Yellow-fruited types are 'Golden Boy' (globe-shaped fruit with a low acid content), 'Yellow Pear' (small pear-shaped fruit; mild flavor), 'Yellow Plum' (2-inch long, oval fruit; sweet flavor).

Orange-fruited types are 'Burpee's Jubilee' (bright golden orange fruit with low acid; very productive), 'Sunray' (fusarium wilt resistant).

Pink-fruited types are 'Oxheart' (large fruit, up to 1 lb.; few seeds), 'Ponderosa' (flattened fruit; mild flavored).

Processing types are 'Heinz 1350' (suitable for canning), 'Roma' (plum-shaped fruit used for tomato paste or canning), 'San Marzano' (rectangular-shaped fruit that stores well; good for canning or tomato paste).

Standard-fruited tomatoes produce broad, meaty, tasty fruit on large vines in about 3 months after planting. Early types are 'Earliana' or 'Spark's Earliana' (heavy producer), 'Early Girl', 'Easy Peel Hybrid' (fruit can be peeled without scalding), 'Spring Giant Hybrid' (heavy producer), 'Springset' (performs well in the North, Midwest, East, and Oregon). Midseason types are 'Better Boy Hybrid' (VFN; foliage protects fruit from sun scald), 'Burpee's VF Hybrid' (good crack resistance), 'Patio' (medium-size plant good in containers). Late types are 'Ace 55 VF', 'Beefsteak' (extra large fruit with prominent ribbing; low acid content), 'Big Boy'.

How to plant. The choice of tomato varieties in stores is often limited. Send away early for seeds, and start them indoors 6 weeks before frost danger is past. Harden off tomato plants, including purchased plants, before setting them into the garden. Tomatoes cannot withstand frost; wait until late spring to transplant into the garden.

Dig in a bushel of compost or rotted manure for each plant, mulch with straw or plastic, and feed with a complete fertilizer. Some of the heaviest yields recorded have been made with the full-season, controlled-release fertilizers.

Set plants out in a sunny spot when they are 6 to 10 inches tall, 24 to 48 inches apart. Work a complete fertilizer into the planting bed according to label directions. Set the plants in deeply — you can bury as much as half to three quarters of the leafless part of the stem. Roots will form along the buried part of the stem and make the plants grow stronger.

To save space and make tomato growing easier, install stakes before you plant. Unstaked vines will sprawl across many square feet and some fruits will lie on the soil, often causing rot, pest damage, and discoloration. A 6-foot-long stake (at least 1-by-1 inch) driven into the ground at least a foot from each seedling is the simplest method to install. A cylinder of welded wire is more trouble to install but makes it easier to train vines. Put stakes at opposite sides of each cylinder and tie it firmly to them. Poke vine branches into openings in the cylinder as the plant grows. (Other staking ideas are on page 21.)

Care. Cut off the suckers that form between the branches and main stem to open up vines and to encourage opening of fruit.

Irrigate tomato plants frequently during the early part of the season, less frequently after fruit begins to set.

Tomatoes will pollinate reliably at 65° for late varieties, at 60° for early varieties. Fruit-setting hormones are worth the expense where summer nights are cooler.

Tomatoes should be watered deeply at least every 10 days during dry spells. Blossom drop can be caused by too much or too little water or not enough sun.

Pests. Tomato hornworms, though bizarre and menacing looking, won't harm you and can be picked off by hand. Whiteflies can gather in great numbers underneath leaves without doing much damage. Blights, viruses, and wilts are usually the reasons for mysterious shriveling and death. Look for streaks, blotches, curly tops (some curling is normal). Pull out sick plants and try disease-resistant varieties next time.

Harvesting. For fresh use, harvest at the stage of ripeness that most appeals to you. For juice or canning, fruit can remain on the vine for several days past the best harvest stage while you are waiting for enough fruits to ripen to make preserving worthwhile. Large green tomatoes will ripen in several weeks in a cool, humid dark place (around 60°).

In containers. Although any tomato plant can grow in a large enough container, the dwarf varieties are best suited for pots with a soil capacity of 1 cubic foot (recommended varieties, page 73). Provide tubs with a capacity of 3 cubic feet for standard-size plants. Set stakes in the soil at the time of planting and tie foliage to them as it grows. Small-fruited cherry and pear tomatoes are ideal for hanging baskets (see page 28). Tomatoes are well suited to hydroponic culture (see page 33); in some areas they are hydroponically grown as a commercial crop.

Left: *Remove suckers to redirect energy from growth to fruit.* **Right:** *Plant seedlings deep; up to half of stem can be buried.*

Turnips and Rutabagas

Plant turnip seeds to harvest in spring, or fall; rutabaga seeds for fall and winter harvest.

Left: *turnip.* **Right:** *rutabaga*

These cool-season, frost-hardy cousins produce huge crops of edible roots and greens. Both spring and fall crops of turnips are possible, but rutabagas are almost always planted in midsummer for a late fall harvest. Turnips require 45 to 60 days to mature roots; rutabagas, 90 days. The heavy tops of rutabagas are edible but coarse. Turnip greens are very popular, cooked alone or mixed with diced or sliced turnip roots or in equal parts with mustard greens.

Turnip plants can reach about 18 inches in height and spread but can be spaced closely for intensive gardening. Rutabaga plants are much larger and are generally widely spaced to allow the large roots to reach their full weight of 3 to 5 pounds each. Rutabaga roots can be kept in cool storage if washed, trimmed, dried thoroughly, and dipped in wax.

Different varieties give a nice choice of colors and shapes. Turnips can be globe shaped or flattened globe. Colors are white, white topped with purple, or creamy yellow. Rutabagas have large yellowish roots, sometimes topped with purple.

Recommended varieties. Turnips for roots and greens: 'Golden Ball', 'Just Right Hybrid', 'Purple Top White Globe', 'Seven Top' (used for greens only), 'Shogoin' or 'Foliage' (can be used for greens in about 30 days, roots in 70 days), 'Tokyo Cross Hybrid' (roots will grow to 6 inches in diameter without becoming pithy; resistant to disease and virus). Rutabagas: 'Altasweet', 'American Purple Top Yellow', 'Laurentian'.

How to plant. Work plant food into the bed and broadcast a second application around plants a month later. For spring crops, plant seeds ¼ inch deep in short rows as early in the spring as the soil can be worked. For fall harvest, sow seeds ½ inch deep in midsummer. Broadcast turnip seeds or sow them thinly in rows 18 inches apart. Sow rutabaga seeds 1 to 2 inches apart in rows 30 inches apart. Thin seedlings to 4 to 8 inches apart.

Care. During dry weather, two or three waterings per week will be needed to prevent wilting of foliage.

Pests. Control root maggots on summer-planted crops with diazinon in the furrow before planting seeds. If they persist, don't plant during warm weather. Control aphids and cabbage loopers with malathion. Follow label directions when applying chemicals.

Harvesting. Pick greens while they are the size of your hand or smaller; the stems of older leaves get stringy. Begin pulling turnip roots when they reach 2 inches in diameter. Roots will keep in the ground until the soil begins to freeze solid. Then they can be dug and topped and stored in a straw or leaf pile or a very cool root cellar. Pull and top rutabagas before roots are injured by extreme cold.

In containers. Both these root crops require a great deal of soil depth to be successful. Try kohlrabi instead — it's prettier, grows faster, and produces its crop above ground.

Quick and easy planting chart (See next three pages)

In this chart you'll find the general information needed for planning your garden. When the time comes to plant, look for more detailed information under each vegetable listed in the Gardener's Guide, pages 34–75.

The first three columns show the recommended method for planting —indoors in containers or outdoors in the ground — as well as the season to plant. If information appears in the first column, this means that planting seeds indoors or in a hotbed (see page 14) is recommended for starting that vegetable. The second column tells you when to transplant your own seedlings or plants bought at the nursery. (Rely on indoor planting where the growing season is very short and you need a head start or when seeds are very small and the outdoor germination rate is low.)

Columns three through seven give information on planting seeds outdoors. In column eight, the distance between transplants/seedlings applies to both setting out plants and thinning seedlings.

The time needed for seeds to sprout will vary with the soil temperature. Use harvest date information for general planning only — it will vary with the variety planted, your locality, and time of sowing.

Vegetable	Weeks before last frost to plant seeds indoors	Set out transplants	Plant seeds outdoors	Days from planting to sprouting	Soil temperature for starting seeds	Depth to plant seeds	Distance apart to plant seeds	Distance between transplants/seedlings	From seed to harvest (*From setting out transplant)	Comments
Artichokes	N	Early spring-midsummer	N	N	N	N	N	4'	1 yr.*	Perennial. Grow from plants or roots.
Asparagus	N	Fall, winter, early spring	N	N	N	N	N	1-2'	2 yrs.*	Perennial. 3 yrs. from seed. Grow from plant or roots.
Beans										
Bush snap	N	N	Midspring-early summer	7-14	65-75°	1"	3"	4-6"	50-60 days	All beans need warm weather.
Pole snap	N	N	Midspring-early summer	7-14	65-75°	1"	3"	1'	60-70 days	Produce over a longer period.
Bush lima	N	N	Early-midsummer	14-21	70-80°	1"	4"	1'	65-75 days	Need long, warm summers.
Pole lima	N	N	Early-midsummer	14-21	70-80°	1"	6"	1'	80-95 days	Where warm season is short, start indoors in peat pots.
Beets	N	N	After frost-fall	14-21	65-75°	½"	1"	3"	46-65 days	No tolerance for hot weather.
Broccoli	5-7	After frost, late summer-fall	Early spring, midsummer	7-14	60-75°	½"	1"	16"	50-90 days*	Cool weather only.
Brussels sprouts	4-6	After frost, late summer-fall	Late summer-fall	7-14	60-75°	½"	3"	3'	80-90 days*	Cool weather only.
Cabbage	5-7	After frost, late summer	Midsummer	7-14	60-75°	½"	3"	1-2'	50-80 days	Cool weather only.
Chinese cabbage	N	N	Midsummer	7-14	60-75°	½"	3"	1'	65-80 days	Cool weather only. Do not transplant.
Carrots	N	N	Early spring-fall	14-21	65-75°	½"	½"	2"	65-75 days	Keep seedbed moist. Prefer cool weather.
Cauliflower	5-7	After frost, late summer-fall	N	7-14	60-75°	½"	3"	18-20"	60-100 days*	Cool weather only.
Celery	10-12	After frost, late summer	N	14-21	65-75°	⅛"	1"	6"	100-135 days*	Cool weather only.
Chard, Swiss	N	N	Early spring-late summer	14-21	65-75°	½"	1"	12"	45-60 days	Tolerates summer heat.
Collards	N	N	Mid-late spring, late summer-fall	7-14	60-75°	½"	1"	18-24"	75-85 days	Spring planting only in North.
Corn										
Early	N	N	Early-late summer	7-14	55-70°	1"	2"	6"	60-65 days	Plant where warm season is short.
Mid-season	N	N	Early-midsummer	7-14	60-80°	1"	3"	8"	65-80 days	Medium-size ears.

N = not recommended or applicable.

Vegetable	Weeks before last frost to plant seeds indoors	Set out transplants	Plant seeds outdoors	Days from planting to sprouting	Soil temperature for starting seeds	Depth to plant seeds	Distance apart to plant seeds	Distance between transplants/seedlings	From seed to harvest (*From setting out transplant)	Comments
Corn (cont'd.) **Late**	N	N	Early summer	7-14	60-80°	1″	4″	12-18″	80-90 days	Usually larger plants and ears.
Cress	N	N	Early-mid-spring	7-14	60-75°	½″	1″	3″	45 days	Watercress grows 50 days to harvest.
Cucumbers	N	N	Early-midsummer	7-14	70-80°	1″	2-3″	12″	55-65 days	Warm weather only.
Eggplant	8-9	Midspring-early summer	N	14-21	75-80°	¼″	½″	3′	65-80 days*	Indoors, plant 8-10 weeks before last frost.
Endive	N	N	Early spring, late summer	14-21	65-75°	¼″	1″	12-18″	65-90 days	Prefers cool weather.
Garlic	N	N	Early spring, winter	7-14	60-75°	1″	2″	3″	80-90 days	Grow from sets (cloves).
Horseradish	N	Fall, late winter, early spring	N	14-28	N	N	N	1′	9 months*	Plant roots 2″ below soil surface.
Jerusalem artichoke	N	Fall, early spring	N	14-28	N	N	N	10-18″	9-11 months*	Plant tubers 2-4″ deep.
Kale	N	N	Early spring, late summer	7-14	60-75°	½″	1″	6-12″	60-70 days	Tolerates frosts.
Kohlrabi	N	N	Early-late spring, late summer-fall	7-14	60-75°	2″	6″	12″	55-65 days	Use greens from thinnings.
Leeks	10-12	Early summer, late summer	Mid-late spring	14-21	60-75°	¼″	½″	3-4″	80-90 days*	Dislike temperature extremes.
Lettuce Head	3-5	After frost	Late summer-fall	14-21	55-65°	½″	½″	1′	80-95 days	Needs long, cool season.
Leaf	N	N	Early-late spring, late summer-fall	14-21	55-65°	½″	1″	6″	40-45 days	Takes more heat than other lettuce types.
Romaine	N	N	Late summer-fall	14-21	55-65°	½″	½″	8″	70-85 days	Tolerates some heat.
Melons (Except watermelons)	3-4	Mid-late spring	Early-midsummer	14-21	75-80°	1″	4″	3-8′	80-95 days	Indoors, plant in peat pots. Need long, warm season.
Mustard greens	N	N	Early spring, late summer-fall	7-14	60-75°	½″	2″	2′	35-60 days	Prefer cool weather.
Okra	N	Early summer	Early mid-summer	14-21	70-80°	1″	12″	3′	50-60 days	Soak seeds before planting.
Onions Bunching (Green)	N	N	Early spring-fall	14-21	60-75°	¼″	½″	1″	60-75 days	Harvest 25-50 days from plants.

N = not recommended or applicable.

Vegetable	Weeks before last frost to plant seeds indoors	Set out transplants	Plant seeds outdoors	Days from planting to sprouting	Soil temperature for starting seeds	Depth to plant seeds	Distance apart to plant seeds	Distance between transplants/seedlings	From seed to harvest (*From setting out transplant)	Comments
Onions *(cont'd.)* **Bulbing (Dry onions)**	6-8	After frost	After frost	14-21	60-75°	¼″	½″	4″	100-120 days	Harvest 50-70 days from sets.
Parsley	8-10	After frost-late spring, late summer	Early-late spring	21-28	65-75°	¼″	½″	18″	70-90 days	Biennial. Soak seeds before planting.
Parsnips	N	N	Mid-late spring, fall	21-28	60-75°	¼″	½″	6″	100-120 days	Takes frost.
Peas	N	N	After frost, fall	7-14	50-60°	1″	2″	3″	60-70 days	Cool weather only.
Peppers	8-10	Midspring-early summer	N	14-21	70-80°	⅛″	1″	18″	60-80 days	Start 8-10 weeks before transplanting time.
Potatoes	N	N	Early spring, late summer	7-14	N	N	N	18″	90-105 days	Plant sets.
Pumpkins	N	N	Early-midsummer	7-14	65-75°	1″	3″	3′	100-120 days	Warm weather only.
Radishes	N	N	Early spring-fall	7-14	45-70°	½″	1″	1″	20-50 days	Plant winter varieties in the fall.
Rhubarb	N	After frost	N	N	N	N	N	4-6′	2 yrs. 1 yr. from roots	Plant roots in early spring. Perennial.
Rutabaga	N	N	Mid-late spring, late summer	7-14	50-65°	½″	1″	1′	90 days	Best as a fall crop.
Salsify	N	N	Mid-late spring	14-21	65-75°	½″	2″	6″	120-150 days	Will store in ground in winter.
Spinach	N	N	After frost, late summer	7-14	40-55°	½″	1″	8″	40-50 days	Prefers cool weather.
Squash **Summer**	N	N	Early-midsummer	7-14	65-80°	1-2″	2″	4′	50-60 days	Warm weather only.
Winter	N	N	Early-midsummer	7-14	65-80°	1-2″	3″	6-8′	80-120 days	Pick before frost.
Tomatoes	6-8	Midspring-early summer	N	14-21	75-80°	¼″	2″	2-4′	55-90* days	Match variety to climate. Try hybrids.
Turnips	N	N	Early-late spring, late summer	7-14	50-65°	¼″	1″	6″	35-60 days	Prefer cool weather.
Watermelon	2-3	After frost	Early-midsummer	7-14	70-75°	1″	2″	6-8′	70-90 days	Indoors, plant in peat pots.

N = not recommended or applicable.

Index

A handy metric conversion chart

To Change	To	Multiply by
inches (in.)	centimeters (c)	2.54
feet (ft.)	meters (m)	0.3048
yards (yd.)	meters (m)	0.914
ounces (oz.)	grams (g)	28
pounds (lb.)	kilograms (kg)	0.45
fluid ounces (fl. oz.)	milliliters (ml)	30
pints (pt.)	liters (l)	0.47
quarts (qt.)	liters (l)	0.95
gallons (gal.)	liters (l)	3.8
Fahrenheit temperature (°F)	Celsius temperature (°C)	.55 after subtracting 32